Po

Speckled Trout
and
Redfish

Upper Texas Coast Edition
Port Arthur—Galveston—Matagorda—Port O'Connor

George Mason and Greg Cubbison

9 780884 156277

50995

Lone Star Books
A Division of Gulf Publishing Company
Houston, Texas

This book is dedicated to our wives, Toni and Linda, who have demonstrated time and again why we are lucky to have them. They understand our need to be part of the great outdoors, and that makes them very special.

Pocket Guide to Speckled Trout and Redfish
Upper Texas Coast Edition
Port Arthur—Galveston—Matagorda—Port O'Connor

Library of Congress Cataloging-in-Publication Data

Meason, George.
    Pocket guide to speckled trout and redfish: upper Texas coast. Port Arthur, Galveston, Port O'Connor/George Meason, Greg Cubbison.
        p.   cm.
    ISBN 0-88415-627-3
    1. Spotted seatrout fishing—Texas.   2. Channel bass fishing—Texas.   3. Fishing—Texas.   4. Spotted seatrout—Texas.   5. Channel bass—Texas.   I. Cubbison, Greg.   II. Title.
SH691.S66M43   1989
799.1'755—dc20
                                                    89–13270
                                                    CIP

Maps in chapter 4 and on the cover are reproduced from NOAA National Ocean Service chart #11300. Interested persons should contact the National Ocean Service, Riverdale, Maryland 20737-1199, or an authorized NOS dealer for accurate, up-to-date NOS charts. Gulf Publishing Company and the authors do not guarantee the accuracy or currency of the portions of the NOS chart published herein.

The spelling of various coastal place names reflect common usage as determined by NOS charts and *The Handbook of Texas: A Supplement, Vol. III*, edited by Eldon Stephen Branda, Austin, Texas State Historical Association, 1976.

CONTENTS

FOREWORD

Speckled trout and redfish are the most important saltwater fish in Texas, and the principal problem of locating and catching them is that the average angler simply does not have time or experience to know enough of the specifics of how, when, and where to do so. To know these things requires years of experience and many an hour of sometimes fruitless searching for subtle signs and signals that would be missed by less observant eyes.

George Meason and Greg Cubbison obviously have paid their dues, and this latest edition of their handy book is crammed with tips and suggestions relating to specific areas, with detailed descriptions of the waters covered.

Although some old salts (and I'm one of them) may not totally agree with all their opinions on certain tackle items, at least they are not in the least bit vague. They provide the beginner with a clear idea of what the authors believe to be best, right down to the product name and model number.

Meason and Cubbison obviously have done a lot of bay fishing and have caught a lot of fish. Reading this book is in some respects much like having a favorite pair of uncles on the water with you, to learn from and to refer to when questions arise. It would be surprising if they were not opinionated.

They don't just say when or where things happen, but also why. And that is very important because it helps the new angler learn to make his own judgments in constantly changing tides, weather, and fishing circumstances.

The Texas Coast is a complex and vast area of water, and no book can open all its secrets nor guarantee catching fish. But this one can surely offer a head start.

Bob Brister

PREFACE

In late 1987 we wrote the *Pocket Guide for Speckled Trout and Redfish: Galveston Bay System Edition*. This book was written as a reference guide to fishing in the Galveston area and was the only book ever published that discussed the specifics of fishing an individual area. Its intended audience was the beginning saltwater fisherman who wanted to know more about his sport. At various boat and fishing shows we met many of the people who purchased and enjoyed the book. Frequently, their first question was, "When are you going to write about Matagorda?" or Port Mansfield or the Laguna Madre. The answer is now!

The *Pocket Guide to Speckled Trout and Redfish: Upper Texas Coast Edition* and its companion volume, *South Texas Coast Edition*, are the result of these questions. *The Upper Texas Coast Edition* covers the coast from Sabine Pass to Port O'Connor, describing each of the bays in the Galveston Bay System (in a completely new and expanded section), East and West Matagorda Bay, and the Port O'Connor area, including Pass Cavallo and the "back bays." The *South Texas Coast Edition* starts at Port O'Connor and includes the areas of Rockport, Port Aransas, Corpus Christi, Port Mansfield, Port Isabel, and the entire Laguna Madre.

Like our first book, the *Upper Texas Coast Edition* and *South Texas Coast Edition* discuss the specifics of each individual area, as well as when to fish, what to use, how to do it, and why. When you fish, you are trying to catch a specific fish; the ones that are in the area in which you are fishing. It is impossible to catch a general fish. We wrote this book with that idea in mind.

We have fun when we fish and we had fun writing these books. We hope that you enjoy reading them and that you are successful on the water.

George Meason

Greg Cubbison

CHAPTER 1

TECHNIQUES: HOW TO FISH

WADING

Wadefishing is more than what you do if you do not have a boat. It is also more than fishing while standing in the water. Wading is an extremely effective technique for catching fish in shallow water. And, yes, fish do frequent shallow water. The most difficult times to catch fish while wading are during the hottest and the coldest months of the year, usually August and February. During these months, the water temperature does not fall within the comfort zones of the fish. (Additional information on the preferred water temperatures of speckled trout and redfish can be found in Chapter 3.) Spring and fall are the most productive, and the most comfortable, times to wade. Success in wadefishing is dependent upon understanding your wading environment, the variables that affect it, and how to make these conditions work to your advantage.

Why do fish go into shallow water? Incoming tides bring shrimp and small finfish—bait to fisherman, food to other fish—in from the Gulf. As the tide spreads out over the flats, the bait goes with it. Predators, including speckled trout and redfish, follow the bait. With the other variables (such as water temperature and water clarity) equal, it is

1

easier for the predators, including waders, to catch a meal in 3 feet of water than in 6 feet of water.

Do you only wadefish during high tides? No, during an outgoing tide, especially during the first hour or so after the tide changes from a standing high tide, the wader's emphasis changes from the flats to the adjacent guts, cuts, and mouths of bayous. As the water level starts to drop, the bait leaves the flats, bayous, ditches, and coves where the rising tide had carried them. Ambush points for the wader then become the guts that lead to deeper water, and the mouths of the bayous and ditches that lead the bait into the salt-grass marshes.

Do you just wade out as far as you can and start fishing? Once again, no. As a wader, you became a part of the fish's environment. Your success depends upon the degree to which you can remain unnoticed. Noise should be kept to an absolute minimum. This means entering the water quietly, whether from a boat or the shore. Mobility is the key to successful wadefishing. The wader is actively *hunting* for the fish in the true sense of the word. The wader must use all of his senses to locate fish.

Moving as a wader is not walking; it is shuffling your feet slowly across the bottom. This accomplishes three things. First, it moves you through the water slowly and quietly. Second, it allows you to find the random junk, holes, unmarked crab traps, etc., so that you can step over or around them instead of tripping over them and falling on your face. This latter option is extremely disconcerting when you are wearing waders, and a neverending source of joy and delight to your unaffected wading companions (unless, of course, the group was catching fish prior to your unscheduled entry into the water). Third, and to anyone who has been so affected most important, shuffling your feet allows you to gently nudge stingrays out of your way. Stepping on a stingray is an unbelievably painful experience, or so we are told, and one that should be avoided at all costs.

Now that you are in the water, shuffling quietly, where do you go? Assuming that visible bait activity and bottom conditions are the same to either side, the next two considerations are the directions of the tide and the wind. Fish feed into the current, looking for something to be brought to them by the tide. If they do not find anything, it is then easy for them to swim with the tide to change locations. Ideally, you want to retrieve your lure, or allow your bait to float, with the current.

Note the bottom conditions as you are wading. Hard sand is preferred by the fish as well as the fisherman, fortunately. Shell should be noted also, as shell is used by both speckled trout and redfish as a preferred hunting ground. If you are in mud, you should always walk upcurrent to avoid fishing in the mud stirred up by your shuffling.

As an adjunct to your mobility, the ability to make long casts is crucial. The mission is to effectively cover as much water as necessary to find fish. The wind is an extremely important factor in casting. Cast with the wind whenever possible. Casting into the wind can reduce your casting distance by half, meaning that you have to work twice as hard to cover the same area. Put the wind at your back if at all possible.

Live bait or artificials? Most serious wadefisherman use artificials because an area can be worked faster and more effectively with artificials than with live bait. However, live bait is generally preferred by fish, and therefore fishermen, in late July and August when the water is warmer. Bait can be fished under popping corks or on the bottom, depending, again, on where you think the fish will be. On the flats, in waist-deep or deeper water, use corks. Set up your wade to use the tidal movement and winds to let your cork slowly drift over the flat while you walk behind. In shallow water adjoining marshes and in deep guts with fast-moving water, use fish-finder rigs on the bottom. The fish-finder rig is discussed in detail in the next chapter.

Because you are "hunting" fish, look for tell-tale signs. Most waders key upon bait fish activity in the water. Jumping mullet are an indication that bait is in the area; however, what you want, ultimately, is fish not bait. Therefore, what you are looking for is "nervous water," a rippled surface condition caused by a school of mullet that has been crowded together near the surface of the water by a school of predators. Mullet casually swimming by, jumping every once in a while, are a sure sign that what you are looking for is not in the area. Keep shuffling. Slicks and birds (pages 7–11) can also pinpoint fish for the observant wader. Moving grass blades in a marsh, a single jumping shrimp, a gull sitting on the water, a gull hovering over a spot in the water, and sandy streaks in previously clear water are all signs that can pinpoint high-percentage fishing locations to the knowledgeable wader. Always watch for signs.

Fish are affected by sunlight, and affected differently at different times of the year. A bright sun warming a flat in February draws the fish to the warm water, but has the opposite effect on most fish when it happens in July. With all other things equal, wading is most effective in low-light conditions. Early morning, late evening, and night are the prime times to wade. Night wading is discussed in Chapter 7. Wading hardware is discussed in Chapter 2, and the effects of tide, wind, and water temperature are discussed in detail in Chapter 3.

Wading from a boat allows access to many more choice wading locations than are available to the wader who goes fishing in his Blazer instead of his Boston Whaler. Remember, however, stealth is still the name of the game. Engine noise, clanking anchors, dropped tackle boxes, and tossed beverage cans are noises that are transmitted directly to the fish. Sound travels through water five times faster and farther than it does through air. It may require fifteen minutes for fish to calm down and resume feeding after you drive in with your big motor. Cut the motor early, and quietly drift into the area where you will anchor the boat and wade. If there is any significant current, leave someone in the boat who can drive it back if the anchor does not hold. Also, be aware of the tide and what is going to happen while you are fishing. Many people have spent the night in Pringle Lake because a falling tide left their boat high and dry while they were wading.

Wading for speckled trout and redfish involves all of the senses. Do not forget that the spectacular sunrise or sunset that you enjoyed was an added bonus, limit one each per day. Pay attention, move slowly, fish early and often, be courteous, and most of all, enjoy being there.

DRIFTING

Drift fishing is more than fishing from a boat that is not anchored. To be accomplished properly (meaning successfully), you must know your prey and its habits, have an understanding of the tides and wind and the effects of both on the fish, and, finally, have some knowledge of the bottom conditions and water depth over which you will drift.

Drifting is the best way to locate fish on the bays. Using the basic knowledge of wind, water temperature, and tides, you can determine an area to fish. That area should have some structure that will attract fish. Examples of these include reefs, guts, flats, well pads, and hard sand flats. The drift is the method for locating fish within the structure.

as you can cover a large area and are more likely to find fish than if you were stationary.

Drifting is best when the wind and current are going in the same direction. The wind and current move you in search of fish, while you cast with the wind ahead of the boat. Casting with the wind allows for extra distance, as always a very important factor to inshore saltwater fishermen. Most experienced drift fisherman use artificials ahead of the drift. You can also drag live bait behind the boat from an unattended rod anchored in a rod holder. Finger mullet, pinfish, or small croakers are preferred bait; shrimp usually fall prey to bait stealers. Fishing with shrimp can be done by using a cork or by fishing near the bottom. At times, the drag rod is more trouble than it is worth because of hangups on shell, vegetation, or trash. At other times, it can keep you very busy catching the fish that you just drifted over.

Drifting can be an endless, mind-dulling game of chunk and wind, chunk and wind, punctuated suddenly by contact and head-shaking resistance stripping line off your reel. Veteran hardware chunkers understand this and maintain adequate concentration so as not to miss that first strike.

Once the fish are located, a number of options exist, among which are to anchor, drift through and return, or anchor and wade. We prefer not to anchor where the fish are located. The only way anchoring can work is if you are able to get the anchor out without scaring away the fish. Keep in mind that it is more likely that you will bang the anchor and chain in and on the boat, then drop the anchor with a loud splash, and trip and knock over a drink can onto the deck while falling over a tackle box. It's preferable to toss out a drift buoy and keep fishing.

Buoys are absolutely the best method for marking a location. Presumably, it is possible to look for stakes, crab trap buoys, or land references, and be able to return to the spot, but unless the above-water landmarks are really close to where you want to be, using a buoy is much more reliable. Buoys are commercially manufactured or can be homemade, like James Plaag's blue Snowy bleach bottle. Buoys can draw a crowd, so their use is best limited to semi-isolated drifting, not Hannas Reef on a Saturday in June.

Back to the drift-through-and-return idea. The marker buoy should be put out when you catch the first fish of the desired species. The drift should continue until you have gone at least 100 yards past the last strike. Then you should crank the motor and gently move out of the area and circle back toward the marker, avoiding all submerged structure, which might hold fish, and all other boats. Cut the motor and position the boat approximately 100 yards upcurrent from where the fish were previously.

If subsequent drifts indicate that the fish are holding, accompanied by nervous water or slicks, anchoring may be appropriate. By then, everyone involved should know how and when to covertly transfer the anchor from the boat to the bottom. The anchor should be connected to the side cleat on the upwind side of the boat. This will allow everyone the chance to fish out of the side of the boat. When the fish stop biting, pull the anchor and drift or circle and return, whichever looks best.

Another option is to anchor and wade. This can be done from the shoreline or while drifting a reef. Several bays have wadeable reefs. Reef wading is best done by wading the edge and casting onto the reef or into the drop-off adjacent to the reef. Always be aware that walking on shell causes noise, and noise spooks fish. When you leave a reef, the same attention to noise control should be used as if your intention was to circle and drift back through. Motor away slowly until clear of structure and all other boats before resuming planing speed.

Drift fishing is work, but it is a very productive method for locating fish. Most fisherman use this technique. All who do must continuously be aware of other boats and treat each boat with courtesy and respect. If everyone did that, just think how much more fun Hannas Reef and Greens Cut could be at 10:00 on a Saturday morning.

ANCHORING

Fishing at anchor sounds simple. The technique comes in when deciding where to anchor, and in positioning the boat in the desired location without driving the fish out of the county. The decision to fish a specific location is, again, one of tide, wind, water temperature, and the presence of structure to hold the fish.

When anchoring in a potentially dangerous situation, such as near a major pass or jetty system, do not turn the motor off until you confirm that the anchor has caught and is holding. In most, if not all, other situations, the motor should be cut and the final distance covered by drifting or coasting without power. You should have the anchor ready to be quietly lowered into the water, without banging the anchor or chain against the boat or rail.

What do you do when you realize that the guy in the other boat whom you have watched catch six nice speckled trout to your two sheepshead and one croaker, is your next-door neighbor, and he is waving to you to anchor next to him? Obviously, what you do not do is motor in next to him and throw your anchor overboard with a loud splash, at least not if you want to avoid a range war at the old hacienda! What you should do is first, note where his anchor is and how his boat is riding in relationship to the current and the wind. Next, position your boat so that the current and wind will drift you into the desired position. Gently lower your anchor and confirm that it is holding, then play out your anchor rope until you are in the desired position, and, finally, tie it off. To leave the area while he is still fishing, reverse the steps. Quiet, smooth ingress and egress; one of the characteristics of a knowledgeable and courteous human being and fisherman.

When anchoring on a reef or shell pad, the direction of the tidal flow is of major concern. Fish use reefs to feed in the same way that we clean crumbs off a table. The tidal flow washes shrimp and bait fish over and across the hard surface of the reef. Predators wait on the downcurrent edge to feed on these as they are washed off the reef. In other words, fish the downcurrent edge of the reef or shell pad for speckled trout and redfish. (Sheepshead are frequent tenants of the middle of the pads around the existing structure.) Well pads in 6 to 8 feet or more of water can be motored up to without major concern for spooking the nearby fish; however, reefs in less than 5 feet of water must be approached with extreme caution. This is particularly true if redfish are your primary quarry. Redfish will spook more readily than speckled trout in all but the clearest water.

FISHING SLICKS

A "slick" is a sheen on the surface of the water that looks like, and is, a light film of oil. These are caused by fish regurgitating what they have eaten. Fish will do this so that they can continue to participate in a feeding frenzy after they are full, or when they are spooked. Frequently, as you drift up on a slick, several smaller slicks will appear as the boat nears the original slick. These are "fright slicks." Speckled trout, redfish, and large gaff-topsail catfish cause slicks. It should be noted that crab traps can also cause slicks.

Slicks can be located by sight and, more frequently, by smell. The smell is similar to that of watermelon or freshly mowed grass or hay. Once again, awareness of the tidal movement is critical to this technique. This type of fishing is most productive under light wind conditions; that is, a light breeze carries the scent and won't ripple the water to the extent that the slick is dispersed. Since you are actually looking for the fish that cause the slick and not just slicks in general, the size of the slick is important. The desired size is usually described as that of a washtub, or about 2 to 3 feet in diameter and round. Slicks of this size indicate that fish are still in the vicinity.

The depth of the water in which the slicks are located, the wind, and the tidal movement affect where the fish should be in relation to the slick. Slicks found in 10 to 15 feet of water will be farther away from the fish than slicks found in 6 feet or less of water. The slicks take time to reach the surface, and the fish oil is carried by the tides prior to reaching the surface. Slicks appear downcurrent from the fish. Once the slick reaches the surface, it is carried even further away from the fish by the wind and the current.

The key to identifying a fresh slick is the size and shape of the slick. Look for small, round slicks. A long slick is one that has been blown by the wind for some time, and is therefore probably not one that has the fish nearby. Remember that fish feed into the current. If the wind and current are moving in the same direction, the fish should be upwind and upcurrent from the slick. If this is the case, start casting prior to the visible slick. If the current and wind are moving in opposite directions, the high-percentage cast will be directly on the slick.

When a slick is spotted, get at least 100 yards downwind and try to pick up the scent. If there is no scent, it is not a fish slick. If it smells like you just drove past a wrecked watermelon truck, you've got a good one. Next, circle around the slick at moderate RPM, to avoid causing your wake to pass through the area you intend to fish. You should stay at least 100 yards from the slick during this maneuver. When you are upwind of the slick, cut the throttle to idle and move toward it, cutting the big motor 50 yards from the slick. As the momentum of the boat decreases, turn the boat sideways with the lower unit, allowing everyone to fish out of the side of the boat. If you are going to anchor, have the anchor ready and attached to the upwind-side cleat of the boat. Start casting when the big motor is stopped. Do not make noise against the hull of the boat. Most veterans prefer shrimptail jigs in this situation because of the ease in unhooking the fish from the single hook and the ability to immediately recast. Trolling motors are used to fine-tune drifts, and to approach the slick more quickly without the noise of the big motor.

Fishing slicks can be exciting and fast-paced. Again, do not forget courtesy and the rights of the other fisherman. The smell of watermelon means fish to the knowledgeable angler!

FISHING THE BIRDS

"Fishing the birds" is a technique that fishermen use to locate feeding speckled trout by observing the behavior of seagulls. The two primary periods for this type of fishing are in the spring and fall. The spring period begins within a week one way or the other of May 1 (depending upon the weather) and lasts for 6 or 7 weeks. The fall season usually starts in September and extends through November. December and January have also been known to provide excellent fishing under the birds, but not with the consistency of the first two primary periods. However, gulls should always be monitored when on the bays.

How do seagulls locate fish for fisherman? Obviously, locating fish is not the gulls' primary mission. They just happen to like shrimp as much as speckled trout do, and schools of speckled trout drive shrimp to the surface of the water. If a shrimp jumps twice, a gull will be there to catch it. As the shrimp are forced to the surface by the speckled trout, only 2 or 3 seagulls may be there, but in several minutes there may be 15 or 20 gulls circling and diving over the compact school of hapless shrimp.

Speckled trout school by size. Small trout are most commonly found near the surface under the birds. Veterans in search of larger trout will frequently use fast-sinking plugs and jigs in an effort to catch the larger members of the school who work below the smaller trout. More of the larger speckled trout are caught under the birds in the fall than in the spring. Occasionally, redfish and gaff-topsail catfish are also found below schooling specks, taking advantage of the pieces missed by the school above them. Fall is the best time to catch redfish under the speckled trout.

In order to successfully fish the birds, attention to technique is critical. Your approach to the flock of birds will determine whether or not you catch any fish. It is the classic "chicken or feathers" scenario. You must be aware of how your boat will drift and what the wind and current will do to the location of your boat. This must be determined before birds are spotted. Next, find a flock of "working birds." Working birds are a compact group of birds hovering and diving over an area. With birds spotted, the race is on! Planing speed is used to get to the area, but the big motor should be retarded to idle at least 100 yards from the birds. Idle to within 50 yards from the birds, and cut off the big motor. Drift or use a trolling motor to position the boat to the side of the birds. Cast where a bird has just hit the water or where a bird is hovering/looking. The bird can see a fish and is waiting for it to usher a shrimp to the surface. Do not waste time on a misplaced cast. Reel in and cast again. Also, do not stringer or box fish. Throw them on the deck and cast again. Another trick is to have a backup rod available in case of a backlash or tangle. Catch the fish while they are there; they may not be there very long. If someone else is on the birds ahead of you, double the distance of your approach.

The three most common mistakes associated with this technique are rushing up on the birds too quickly and spooking the fish, misaligning the drift (and either drifting into the birds or never getting within effective casting range), and leaving the area as the flock breaks up and flies off. This is not an indication that the fish have left, only that the fish have gone deep and are no longer driving shrimp to the surface. After all, the birds are not fishing; they are shrimping. Stay in the area and fish deep. Remember, the school will feed into the current. You knew where they were earlier, you ought to be able to guess where they have gone. The trick is to reposition the boat without spooking them. In this instance a trolling motor is the answer. Poling will also do the trick, but most anglers are not inclined or equipped.

Not all working birds are fish finders. Pay attention only to the gulls. The smaller terns simulate the gulls' activity but do not produce the same results. They rarely indicate fish. On the bays, terns have many other names, the most common of which is "liar birds." In locating seagulls, binoculars are a must. Focus your attention on the water $1/4$ to $1/2$ mile from the boat, not the sky or the horizon. Birds in the next bay over will have been scattered by other boats by the time you get there.

Everyone who has used this technique has horror stories about some fool crashing "his" flock of birds. Do not be the subject of someone else's similar story. Keep your eyes open, the binoculars close, be courteous, know what you intend to do, be prepared, and follow the gulls to fast-paced action on speckled trout.

CHAPTER 2

EQUIPMENT: WHAT TO USE

Since we fish more often than most people (at least according to our wives), in a single year we can put a piece of equipment through the equivalent of a lifetime of use and abuse. We do not work for any manufacturers, nor do we make a point of trying each new product when it is introduced. What we do is fish a lot, and the equipment that we use is equipment that we bought because it seemed to be able to do what it was that we wanted it to do. We make our recommendations on that basis. Equipment excluded from our list may be excellent; we just have not used it. We do not take anybody else's word for what a product will do. If your favorite rod, reel, or lure is not included in our recommendations, it may be simply because we have not used it.

We use each of the three major types of fishing equipment: bait casting, spinning, and fly. Fly-fishing is an exciting and growing facet of the saltwater fishing scene and will be discussed separately at the end of this chapter.

REELS

Bait Casting

By and large, most of the reels found in use today around saltwater are of the bait-casting variety. The spool shaft of this type of reel is perpendicular to the line, leading some people to refer to them as level-wind. For decades, they have been improved and re-improved until today we have a number of well-thought-out and well-designed reels that are capable of doing what they are supposed to do.

We recommend three reels, each by a different manufacturer. They are as follows:

Model	Line Capacity	Gear Ratio
Shimano BSM-2200WFS	235/12 lb	6:1
Ambassadeur 5500C	195/12 lb	4.7:1
Quantum QD 1420L	200/12 lb	5.1:1

It's difficult to compare these reels because they each have several important features that make them unique. We should first say, however, that their several special features, as well as other manufacturing considerations, set these reels apart as high-quality equipment, proven to be both functional and functioning when it counts.

The Shimano BSM-2200WFS is, for all practical purposes, the same reel as the BSM-2200W. This may be the only thing we can criticize. Several manufacturers seem to feel compelled to make some small change in their product, even though it is in no way necessary. In this case, the model number change did not affect the quality of the product. This reel is made of graphite-composite materials, which have proven themselves to be an absolute godsend on the Gulf Coast. Another important materials consideration is its stainless-steel ball bearings. Design advantages include an extra wide spool for additional line, a 6:1 retrieve ratio, a magnetic spool brake (which helps prevent most backlashes), and a good drag system. There are other appealing features, but the best thing about this reel is the fact that it always seems to perform. And, for some reason, Shimano supplies parts for this model while the same is not true of the spinning models.

Abu Garcias' Ambassadeur 5500C has for years been the choice of many dyed-in-the-wool fishermen on the Gulf Coast. The 5500C has been "Mr. Reliable," the standard by which other reels were measured. Stainless-steel components and ball bearings have made it a dependable performer in saltwater. We remain unconvinced, however, about the new Syncro Drag system as the old drag is still as good as it used to be. Frankly, we cannot understand why they would not spend their money incorporating various space-age composite materials into this fine line of reels.

The feature we like most about the Ambassadeur 5500C is its relatively low retrieve ratio, which allows for a considerable mechanical advantage when playing a trophy fish. Stainless-steel ball bearings are found in all "C" models, which also use dependable oversize brass gears.

Now let's look at a recent contender in the reel competition—Zebco. What's that, you say? Zebco, the Snoopy-reel manufacturer? The 202 of reeldom? Yes, all of the above. You see, someone at Zebco made a decision a few years ago to take a shot at the world of high-end reels. The result was the Quantum line. We have for some time been a fan of the Quantum QSS4, and have touted it as one of the best spinning reels made. Now Zebco, with its Quantum QD 1420L, may have put together a combination of design and materials to top them all. Their choice of materials is a graphite case with stainless-steel components. The drag system, 5.1:1 retrieve ratio, and DynaMag magnetic cast control seem to be the result of an overview of all the most successful features around. If the Quantum line is not on top of the reel business, they sure don't have much company.

Spinning

Many "crusty old salts" (age is not relevant) who think that spinning gear is manufactured solely for women, children, and visiting relatives from Kansas or Nebraska are still alive and well on the Texas coast. We have heard their snickers and comments on those who fish with "pencil sharpeners" or "coffee grinders." We nod politely but disagree.

We match our spinning equipment against any bait caster's equipment in terms of performance and reliability. To us, it is merely a question of preference. That is, until we start discussing casting light lures or free-shrimping into the wind. Then, spinning equipment is the obvious choice. So, if you prefer your spinning reel, use it.

We use GT-X series Shimano reels and Quantum's QSS4. Each of these reels has good points and bad points; however, both are excellent reels and have been used extensively in the saltwater environment.

The GT-X series of reels by Shimano is obviously designed by fishermen for fishermen. They employ many important features to make casting quick and easy. These include a Quickfire II™ trigger for one-hand casting, automatic bail centering, push-button spool removal with line keeper, and a very smooth and reliable rear-mounted drag with Fighting Drag II™. These reels are perfect for the constant casting and retrieving of the hardware enthusiast. A 6.2:1 gear ratio allows the angler to quickly take up the slack in shrimptail jig fishing and to rip MirrOlures and spoons across the flats. This reel has five stainless-steel ball bearings for smoothness. The only problem with this reel is that its gears wear out. You may never wear it out, but we do. Replacement parts can be hard to find. Our last reel was in the shop for 60 days waiting for a part to arrive.

The Quantum QSS4 is another incredibly smooth reel. This reel was designed specifically for saltwater use. It has stainless-steel main gears and center shaft with a metal casing that has an anti-corrosive coating. It features a front-loaded Magnum Drag™ system and a 5.4:1 gear ratio. Initially, some people said that this reel was too small and did not hold enough line. These comments have proven invalid. Quantum did apparently hear these, however, because they came out with a QSS4W that has a wider (thus the "W") spool and holds more line. And, of course, the 4W spool does not fit on a 4. This reel incorporates the Bait Sensor™ switch, which allows the reel to free-spool with the bail closed under easily controlled spool tension. We use this when fishing live bait. The good news is that the reel is unbreakable. We use this reel in the surf where it not only gets wet, but spends considerable time underwater, and with live bait under a cork. For all this abuse, we have not been able to break or wear out this reel. It continues to operate smoothly and reliably. Now for the bad news. The QSS4 does not work well in a fishing environment where slack line is taken up on the reel, as in fishing with shrimptail jigs. Without a small amount of tension on the line as the line is retrieved, the line will fly off the reel in knots on a subsequent cast. We have not tested a QSS4W to determine if the wide spool has resolved this problem. As long as a taut line retrieve is used, the QSS4 is absolutely bulletproof and an excellent saltwater spinning reel.

Maintenance

Periodic maintenance is a logical step to protect the investment you have made in fishing reels. In most boat or bay wading trips, nothing more is required than wiping the salt off the reel and putting it up. If you noticed something stick or bind, check it out and clean, oil, or grease it as required. If, however, your trip included surf fishing or an unscheduled dipping of your reel into the bay, then thorough cleaning and lubrication is required.

Always save the owner's manual for the new reel that you buy. It will contain a diagram of the reel and its parts. This diagram is helpful in subsequent takedowns of the reel. The manual will also suggest areas of periodic maintenance, as well as describe the process required and the tools and materials needed; for example, when to use grease and when to use oil.

When reels have been underwater, first, soak them in warm water for 30 minutes, during which all moving parts should be moved to ensure that the warm water will dissolve all the salt off the reel parts. Next, disassemble the reel and make sure it is cleaned and dried. After the parts have dried, lubricate each part as required, and reassemble the reel. When initially disassembling a reel, work slowly, refer to the owner's manual diagram, and lay out the pieces in the order that they are removed. This will assist you later when the process is reversed. Tools needed to perform most periodic maintenance include two small screwdrivers (one flat, one Phillips), reel oil (We use gun oil to refill our nifty little hypodermic-looking oil droppers. Gun oil will not gum or cake as will WD-40, and you can buy it cheaper and in larger quantities than you can buy real reel oil.), reel grease, and a small crescent wrench. Be careful to use the proper size tool to avoid damaging a part, and avoid overtightening metal screws into plastic housings. In selecting a repair location, ask if they stock parts for your reel or if they have to order them from the distributor. Readily available, in-stock parts are the key to a quicker turnaround on your reel.

RODS

We use 7-foot-long, one-piece graphite rods no matter what type of fishing we are doing. Next time you see a catalog from a major fishing manufacturer, check out the number of one-piece 7-foot graphite rods designed to be used with up to 17-lb test line and up to $3/4$oz lures. We will save you the trouble; most manufacturers do not make such a rod. Fortunately, two manufacturers, LCI and All Star Graphite Rods, Inc., have decided to support the Gulf Coast market by carrying these rods.

If you are going to have a single rod and want to do all kinds of fishing, we recommend the LCI Excelon GPR 704 or the All Star PRM-IM6 in bait casting, and the PRMS in spinning (IM6 is not available in this model). If you use different types of artificials and want to match rods to the specific lure type, we offer the following as our recommendations. For shrimptail jig fishing: LCI Excelon GPR 700 KelleyWiggler Special or the All Star PRL Special-IM6 Shrimptail Special in bait casting. All Star does not offer this rod in spinning. Each of these rods has a shorter handle to facilitate jigging the lure without hitting your chest/chest waders. For all but the heaviest surf spoons and for live bait on a fish-finder rig, we recommend the LCI Excelon GPR 702 and the All Star PRL-IM6 in bait casting and the All Star PRL in spinning (IM6 is not available in this model). For MirrOlures, big spoons, and live bait under a popping cork, we recommend the all-purpose rods discussed. If transporting a 7-foot rod will cause a problem, LCI also makes two-piece models of the 702 and 704, 702-2 and 704-2, respectively. All Star offers a PRM-2 for bait casting (IM6 is not available in this model).

Each of the selected rods, except where noted, are made from IM6 blanks. IM6 carbon fibers have an inherent stiffness, which provides for a lighter, stronger, and more sensitive rod. LCI offers its Striker series of rods (instead of the Excelon series) that are not made of IM6 graphite and, consequently, are less expensive. It should also be noted that Excelon rods have a 3-year limited warranty (Strikers have a 1-year limited warranty) against defects. In most instances, such a warranty would mean little to us. In this case it does. On two occasions we have broken LCI Excelon rods while fishing. Each time the rod was cheerfully replaced without question by the retailer where it was purchased. We still do not read that in the warranty, but that is the way it worked, and that is why we primarily use and recommend LCI products.

TACKLE

Fishing Line

We use Berkley Trilene Big Game 12-lb test line. Before the introduction of Big Game, we used Trilene XL in 14-lb test. We have been extremely pleased with the Big Game, having been able to go to a lighter line without sacrificing anything that could be noticed in the two most important characteristics of our fishing line: strength and abrasion resistance.

Most fishermen equip themselves to catch small speckled trout. As a result of this, most hookups with monster speckled trout result only in great "fish stories" instead of great fish. An 8- to 10-lb speckled trout will inhale any lure that it mistakenly tries to eat, putting its teeth in direct contact with the angler's main line. For this reason, we always use an 8- to 10-inch shock leader of 20-lb test Trilene XL. The leader is attached to the main line using a small black barrel swivel (Rosco #R5F-BL). On the business end, we tie a Berkley Cross-Lok Snap Swivel, size 12 (P12XSB). Size 10 will work, but is almost too large to fit through the eye on a MirrOlure, and is also harder to use with wet hands and waves breaking over your head. The only time that we do not use swivels to attach our lures is when we believe that redfish may be in the area. Redfish can bite the swivel while they are being played, causing it to open, and causing the long-distance release of your fish. This has happened to us on three different occasions. We subsequently wised up!

Live Bait Hooks

When using live bait, we always use treble hooks. We prefer Eagle Claw 3X strong hooks. The most popular live bait is shrimp, both with the fish, because they are a primary food source for speckled trout and redfish when they are small, and with the fisherman, because of their ready availability during the primary fishing season of late spring through the fall. For live shrimp, we use a size 6 treble hook. This hook is the right size for all but the tiniest shrimp, the "whiskers and eyeballs" variety.

Because we spend most of our time in and on the water looking for large fish, we prefer to use live finfish as bait instead of shrimp. This is not to say that you cannot catch large fish on shrimp, or medium-to-small fish on a live finfish. In fact, large shrimp, 4 to 5 inches long, are absolute killers on large speckled trout and redfish; however, these are also table-sized shrimp and are difficult to find in bait shops. We use finger mullet, menhaden (shad), pinfish, and small croakers in this respect. A cast net is required to catch finger mullet and shad. A size 8 treble and a piece of shrimp near the bottom will usually catch a supply of pinfish and croakers. We hook these fish through the lips (more correctly through the lips and into the nose) on a size 4 treble hook. The larger hook is necessary to reach the upper lip of the fish. If you merely hook the lips themselves, after the cast your bait and the rest of your rig will not hit the water in the same area. This is particularly frustrating after you just spent a considerable length of time catching the little sucker. In short, hook your bait deeply to ensure that it remains intact during the cast. While shrimp are the primary forage for immature speckled trout and redfish, when they mature they switch to finfish as their primary food source. It makes sense. Fish are larger; therefore, the predators have to catch and eat fewer finfish to fill up than they would if they were eating shrimp.

Popping Cork

The popping cork is more than simply a way to suspend a bait between the surface and the bottom. The concave upper surface of the cork is designed to scoop water as it is dragged across the surface by quickly jerking the rod tip upward. To the fish, this scoop simulates the sound of a speckled trout taking shrimp off the surface of the water. This faux feeding sound is an attractor to the fish. When you pop the cork, you are calling nearby fish by telling them that other fish in the area have found something to eat, and that they had better get over there before the other fish eat all the shrimp.

Not all popping corks are created equal. As in all saltwater fishing, distance in casting is important. We, therefore, use large cork and weight combinations to enhance our casting distance and to ensure that we can still see the cork after we have thrown it as far as we can. We use 6-inch unweighted corks, oddly enough made out of cork, not plastic. To allow these to float properly, we use a pink $1\frac{1}{2}$-oz swivel-end weight (SE-10) tied onto the line halfway between the cork and the hook. We use 25-lb test line throughout, from the cork to the hook. This heavier line provides extra strength and abrasion resistance to the rig. We also add an additional attraction system to our corks to enhance their effectiveness by putting two plastic $1/4$-inch beads above and below the cork. As the cork is popped and as it settles, these beads click together, simulating the clicking sound made by a shrimp when it is startled.

Now, for the real trick. How is all of this put together in order to do all these wonderful things? This is a three-step process. First, combine the cork and the beads. To do this, tie a number one black swivel to 12 inches of 25-lb test line. Then slide two $1/4$-inch round, pink, plastic beads onto the line. The corks we use are green with day-glow orange tops. They have a hole drilled through them, through which the line is passed. Because of the constant impact of the beads against the bottom of the cork, it will eventually start to crack. To eliminate this, buy a 5-inch cork that comes with a hollow green plastic stem that runs through the cork from top to bottom. Take out the stem and throw the cork away. Take the stem and insert it into the 6-inch cork from the bottom. The base of the stem protruding from the bottom of the cork becomes the shock absorber, preventing damage to the cork.

Now, take your barrel swivel, beads, and line and insert the line through the cork from the top and out the bottom, through the shock absorber stem. (When buying the cork and stem, look through the stem to ensure that it is hollow all the way through.) Next, add two more beads onto the line. Tie another number one black barrel swivel as close as possible to the last two beads. This process gives you a cork on an 8-inch line, with black barrel swivels on both ends, and a pair of beads above and below the cork.

The rigs that we use are fixed-depth models. We rig several of these for different depths. A rig set for 3 feet and one for 5 feet will suffice in most wading or boating situations. For a 3-foot rig, cut two pieces of 25-lb test line approximately 20 to 22 inches in length. Tie the end of one to the barrel swivel at the base of the cork and tie the fixed end of the pink $11/2$-oz swivel-end weight to the other end. Tie one end of the other piece of line to the swivel on the swivel-end weight. (The swivel on the weight will eliminate line twist as the bait is retrieved through the water.) Finally, tie the appropriate treble hook to the other end of the line. The pink weight between the cork and the hook is an attractor, as well as a means to ensure that the current does not force the bait too far away from its intended depth.

As always, casting this rig is easiest when done with the wind. Casting into a strong wind will occasionally cause the bait to tangle with the cork. This is easy to identify because the cork will either not float upright or will not pop properly. This rig is extremely productive and will, more times than not, produce more strikes than other straight popping corks. Catching the fish that hit your bait is up to you.

Fish-Finder Rigs

A fish finder is a very simple and very effective bottom rig. It can be used in any bottom fishing situation, as a stationary tight-line rig in the surf or from a bulkhead or pier, as well as a moving rig retrieved to work an entire area or drifted with the current. Its components are a weight, a number one black barrel swivel, a leader, and a hook. We tie 24 to 30 inches of 25-lb test line to the barrel swivel. The weight is then slid onto the main line and the main line is tied to the other end of the swivel. The hook is tied to the end of the leader opposite the swivel. This rig is most often used with live bait, but can also be used with dead. The amount of weight used is dependent upon whether the bait will be stationary on the bottom or moved along at or near the bottom. We have used this tackle in the surf when the currents dictate using a 5- or 6-oz spider weight. Depending upon the size of the eye on the weight, it is sometimes necessary to put a 1/4-inch round plastic bead onto the main line between the weight and the swivel. Use of a larger swivel will also preclude having the weight stick on or slide completely over the swivel. In most instances in the bays, a 1/4- to 1/2-oz barrel weight will suffice to keep the weight at or near the bottom. It is only in the surf or in close proximity to a pass that additional weight is required.

The theory behind this simple rig is best explained using, for example, a stationary rig in a gut or pass where the current is moving. The weight is on the bottom and the bait is floating in the current near the bottom. Fish feed into the current. Swimming upcurrent, it sees the bait and takes it. Because of the length of the leader between the fish and the weight on the bottom, the fish initially feels no resistance. This provides time for the fish to ingest the bait before becoming aware that something is wrong.

In many instances with a stationary rig, speckled trout will actually set the hook themselves when they run out of slack in the leader. This differs from the typical bottom rigs sold in bait camps and tackle shops everywhere, the kind with two drops for hooks and a third for the weight. With these, because of the shorter drops, the fish has less time to swallow, hence is alerted to the danger sooner and the need to get rid of the bait. Another problem with these rigs is that they have hardware (snap swivels) with which to attach the hooks. These are usually as big or bigger than the hooks. Speckled trout and redfish are not dumb or blind; extra hardware next to your bait does not help your chances of fooling these fish. Their market is dependent upon fisherman who are either lazy or do not know how to tie knots. The fish-finder rig will help you score when the fish are on the bottom.

LURES

Our treatise on saltwater lures will be limited to the basics. The three most common types of hardware used along the coast are mullet/finfish imitations, shrimptail and shad-type jigs, and spoons. A collection of each of these types of lures is in every saltwater veteran's tackle box. The amount of use each of these gets is in direct correlation to the degree of confidence that the angler has in that lure. More than likely, that confidence is a result of the angler's better technique in presenting and working one lure over another. Our point is that lures do not catch fish; skillful, persistent, and knowledgeable fishermen catch fish. If your ability to catch fish with a particular lure is not as accomplished as the person next to you, watch what he or she is doing. We believe that effort is required to be a good fisherman. This is another instance of the validity of the 90/10 rule. Ten percent of the fishermen catch 90 percent of the fish. Those 10 percent are the ones that work at it, work at understanding weather and how it affects fish, work to perfect all of their fishing techniques, and work at learning the areas that they fish. Proficiency comes to those who want it badly enough.

MirrOlures

The MirrOlure, while manufactured in Florida, is a Texas legend. Few, if any, who have ever gotten their feet wet in the Texas surf while holding a fishing pole do not own several MirrOlures. There are five different series of MirrOlures, used to varying degrees by speckled-trout fishermen in Texas. We are sure that others catch redfish on MirrOlures, but not us. To us the MirrOlure is a speckled-trout lure (flounder, too, but this is not about flatfish).

MirrOlures are distinguished from one another by a code, which at first glance, was apparently designed by a rocket scientist. Further investigation reveals a simple code based upon series, Rattler or no, scale color, and body colors. The series is based upon the lure's rated running depth and/or lure configuration. The Rattler is a fish attractor that we believe should be on every MirrOlure purchased. The color combinations are designated by either a 2- or 3-digit number, or in some cases a letter or group of letters. A 3-digit number starting with a 7 has silver side scales. A 3-digit number starting with an 8 has gold side scales. The R (52MR11 as opposed to 52M11) means that it is a Rattler. The 51 series has the eye for attachment to your line in its nose. The 52 series has the eye where we suppose the lure's forehead would be. The TT series is the 52 series with spots, hence the name Tiny Trout. These lures are favorites among wadefishermen, particularly the 51 series. We believe that the 52 series offers more flexibility, as it is easier to keep the 52 shallow than it is to make the 51 run deep using a moderate to fast retrieve. For this reason, unless you plan on owning as many MirrOlures as we do, only buy the 52MR series. MirrOlure also has 2 deep-running lures that we use from a boat in deep water or in fast-moving water as found around the passes. These are the 60 and 65 series. Neither of these deep-water series are available as a Rattler.

As far as color selection, we have several principles that work for us. In extremely clear water, such as you find in the winter, go to whites and silver scales, 52MR51 or 52MR24. In clear green water, throw bright colors with silver scales, 52MR752, 52MR704, or 52MRSHP. In clear tea-colored water, use oranges and blacks with gold scales, 52MR801 or 52MR808. In sandy green water, use reds and yellows with gold scales, 52MR28, 52MR12 or 52MR12FGO.

In deciding scale color, use the same rule that we applied in selecting spoon color. Redfish are predators. Their survival is dependent upon being able to catch food. A redfish caught from clear water will appear very different from one caught in dirty water. The clear-water redfish will be golden. The dirty-water redfish will be silver. In other words, to fish (at least to redfish) gold is less visible in clear water than silver, and vice versa. Use silver scales in clear water and gold scales in off-colored water. Light conditions also affect color selections. In bright sunshine, use bright colors and silver scales; in overcast conditions use dark colors; in first or last light, use black. Tables 1–3 show a specification chart on MirrOlures, a primary list for those starting their MirrOlure collection, and a secondary list for those who still have some leftover money and/or space in their tackle box for a few more excellent lures.

Other Killer Hardware

Bingo lures have been around forever, it seems. Our fathers used them after they returned from WW II. The most popular of these are the King Bingo, $3/4$oz and $3 3/4$inches, the Queen Bingo, $9/16$ oz and 3 inches, the Plugging Shorty, available in two sizes—Small, $5/16$ oz and $2 3/8$ inches and Bull, $9/16$ oz and 3 inches; and the Hump, $9/19$ oz and $2 5/8$ inches. Each of these are fast-sinking, hard plastic lures. The most popular colors are: King Bingo—chrome, Queen Bingo—pink, Plugging Shorty—pearl, smoke, motor oil, and amber, and the Hump—pearl and pink.

Bagley's Finger Mullet has also produced a following on the coast. These lures are slow sinking with two treble hooks. They do not have the authority that some hard plastics do into a strong onshore wind in the surf, but two trebles is three less barbs to stick into your body when things get exciting on the third bar.

Topwater plugs have been used on the coast for over a decade, yet only recently have they migrated up the coast and started to get some

Table 1
MirrOlure Specifications

Series	Depth (ft)	Length (in.)	Weight (oz)
51M	1–4 +	$3^5/8$	$1/2$
52M	1–4 +	$3^5/8$	$1/2$
TT	1–4 +	$3^5/8$	$1/2$
60M	3–6 +	$3^5/8$	$5/8$
65M	10–20 +	$3^3/16$	1

Table 2
Primary MirrOlure Recommendations

		Description	
Color Designation	Top	Scale	Bottom
11	red head; white	silver	white
12	red head; yellow	gold	yellow
28	red	gold	yellow
54	black	silver	black
801	orange	gold	orange
SHP	pink	silver	pink
704 (Texas Chicken)	pink	silver	yellow
752 (Tahiti Sunrise)	orange	chartreuse	yellow
CA	candy-apple red	candy-apple red	candy-apple red
808	black	gold	orange

Table 3
Secondary MirrOlure Recommendations

		Description	
Color Designation	Top	Scale	Bottom
21	black	silver	white
24	blue	silver	white
26	red	silver	white
51	white	silver	white
750	black	chartreuse	orange
12FGO	orange head; yellow	gold	yellow
751	chartreuse	chartreuse	chartreuse
803	pink	gold	pink
807	black	gold	black
809	black	gold	pink

well-deserved publicity. When topwaters are mentioned, most think of the "broken backs." First in popularity among these are the Cotton Cordell Redfins. Bomber's Long A's and Rapala's Jointed Floating Minnows are also proven favorites for large speckled trout and redfish. The retrieve on these lures is the key to success. The two basic techniques used are stop-and-go and a steady retrieve. The speeds will vary. Sometimes a slow steady retrieve, keeping the lure on the surface pushing water ahead of it, draws the strikes. At other times, swimming the lure 12 inches below the surface works. Swimming the lure a foot deep, then stopping and allowing it to float to the surface is another favorite tactic. Obviously, the key is varying your retrieve until something works and then repeating that presentation. If a fish strikes and misses, do not stop the lure. Most veterans believe that stopping the lure will give the fish a chance at a good look at the lure enabling it to recognize it for what it is—a lure, not food. An escaping lure frequently triggers another strike. Favorite colors for these lures are silver/black back, gold/black back, and silver/blue back. Long A's come in a variety of popular colors, with strawberry with a pink tail a favorite. Other popular topwaters are the Zara Spook, Heddon's Tiny Torpedo and Baby Torpedo, Swithwick's Devil's Horse, and Bagley's Chug-O-Lure.

Many saltwater anglers do not realize that topwaters are not only skinny water baits. They can be used effectively in 8 feet of water, especially during a slack tide when normal feeding activity is greatly reduced. Deep water use is usually best when swimming the bait a foot below the surface. Strong tidal flow is, however, not conducive to effective topwater activity. The Bomber Long A is a good deepwater broken back.

Shrimptail/Shad Jigs

KelleyWigglers, or more precisely, the KelleyWiggler Texas Long John, is the king of the shrimptails on the Texas coast. Their 4-inch tail is flexible, durable, and the primary artificial used by a large percentage of coastal fishermen. The tails are, of course, used in conjunction with a lead jig head. KelleyWiggler (Alpha Bait Company) also produces a unique jig head, employing a 3-sided head instead of a round head. This design uses differential water pressure on the surface to add additional action to the lure. Instead of falling straight down like a round head, the KelleyWiggler head will veer to one side or the other. More action means more fish. More action also usually means more effort. This time the extra effort is not required. You just have to use the right jig head. This action is most pronounced in the $3/8$-oz jig head. With the proper rod, this rig can be fished as slowly as a $1/4$-oz jig. KelleyWiggler's most popular colors are strawberry, strawberry cooltail, chartreuse firetail, black, black cooltail, white, and pearl firetail. We prefer strawberry cooltail and chartreuse firetail. There are two basic rules in color selection of KelleyWigglers: Use strawberry/strawberry cooltail in most situations, but use dark colors in trout-green water and bright colors in clear water. We use strawberry cooltail unless the water is very clear; then we prefer the chartreuse firetail. We work these baits using an LCI KelleyWiggler Special rod (GPR 700) using a series of three irregular jerks of the rod tip, then allowing the jig to settle to the bottom while retrieving the slack line. The fish usually strike as the lure settles.

Hogie's $3^{1/2}$-inch Swimming Shad is the leader in the shad-type soft plastic baits. The "club foot" tail of this bait provides for enhanced action in the jigging technique. These are also used effectively under a Mansfield Mauler. Favorite colors are strawberry with a pink tail, and root beer with a pink tail. These lures can be jigged across the bottom or retrieved in a slow, swimming motion, popping the rod tip and allowing the lure to settle every 6 or 8 cranks.

Spoons

We use spoons on a regular basis. We also use several sizes of spoons to match the weather and water conditions. We use silver spoons in clear and green water and bright sunshine, and gold spoons in sandy-green water and low-light conditions. Our $1/2$- and $3/4$-oz spoons are Johnson Sprites. In the surf and in fast-moving water, we use a $1^{1/4}$-oz Tony Accetta spoon in both gold and silver. We frequently use bucktails on our spoons, red on the gold spoon and white on the silver. We put stainless-steel split rings through the eye of the spoon to attach to our shock leaders, when not using swivels, for redfish.

We have a major problem with the hooks and split rings that come from the factory on these spoons. Their average life is about two weeks after they come out of the package. To ensure that our spoons are serviceable, we replace the split rings and hooks with stainless-steel models of each. While in the process of doing this, we also add a piece of pink teaser tube to the shank of the stainless-steel treble hook. We think these are pretty, and the fish must agree. On $1/2$- and $3/4$-oz spoons, we use a number three split ring and a number four treble hook. On the $1^1/4$-oz spoons, we use a number six split ring and a number one treble hook. If your favorite tackle-shop salesman grins at you when you ask him where the stainless-steel treble hooks are, it is because he knows how much they cost and you do not! But, what the heck. This way your spoons will last forever, or until you loose them, whichever happens first. When fishing in or over grass, we use a single hook instead of the grass-grabbing treble.

SPECIAL EQUIPMENT

The sundry equipment that we deem necessary, useful, practical, or merely neat, and is therefore included in our tackle boxes, on our wading belts, or in the boat when we go fishing is discussed in this section. Feel free to pick and choose as you deem appropriate.

When we are wadefishing, we carry lures in plastic lure boxes with separate compartments inside. To facilitate cleaning the lures to pro-long their useful lives, we have drilled holes through the top and bottom of each compartment. When we return from a trip, we submerge these boxes in clean water to dissolve the salt. After they have soaked, we shake out the water, salt, etc., and lean the boxes at an angle, allowing any excess water to drain while the lures dry. This has significantly reduced the frequency of having to replace hooks or discard corroded lures. We either carry these boxes in a fanny pack or drag them on our stringer float, attached by a cord which runs through the hole built into the box for such a purpose. We do not use the styrofoam wading hats because to us they are uncomfortable, clumsy, and tend to be blown off by the wind or knocked off by waves, while providing a stable platform on which rust can eat a fortune's worth of lures.

Wading belts are designed to function as your tackle box while wading. Ours do a good job of it, and more. Along with the standard rod holder and stringer holder into which the point of the stringer is stuck down vertically (this is the best holder we have found), we have added needle-nose pliers (the hardware store, not tackle store, variety), a large hemostat/scissors combination tool, and a small fillet knife. We have also put a 2-inch welded ring on the back of the belt. To this we attach our life vests, using a length of ski rope to which we added snaps at each end. One end snaps to the ring on the belt, the other snaps to a heavy split ring that is inserted into the lacing eyes on the side of the vest. That way nothing gets lost, including us. We carry a short-handled landing net by inserting it into our zipped vest. The ski rope is inserted through the elastic cord on the net to secure it to us. We also make our nets float by taking off the handle and stuffing cork into the hollow frame of the net. Pretty slick, huh?

We have been required to use our life vests on two instances. We are cautious waders and do not take chances; however, we walked places from which we could not walk back. We could have been in something more than deep water without our vests. Instead, we simply laid on our vests and floated along the shoreline until the waves deposited us back on hard sand. We then walked back and continued fishing. The end to the story could have been significantly different, in terms of discarded equipment and stark terror (assuming that we did not drown). As the Boy Scouts say, be prepared (no one plans to have an accident!).

Because we occasionally (make that frequently) pack our vehicles in a mad dash to get to the coast more quickly in order to take advantage of some phenomenon of limited duration such as green incoming/outgoing tide, daylight, calm winds, bird activity, or a known location of fish, we have, at one time or another, forgotten almost every single piece of equipment required to fish. To avoid this humiliating problem, we have made a checklist to remind us what we are supposed to have with us. We have included this checklist for you to use as a basis to make your own. It is found in the Appendix of this book.

Polarized sunglasses with sideshields and a neck cord should be included on everyone's list of critical equipment. Not only will these keep you from being blinded by sunlight reflecting off the water, they will allow you to see things of particular interest in the water such as fish, bait, stingrays, tires, reefs, crab traps, jellyfish, and your line. Your ability to locate these items in the water can have a significant impact upon whether your trip to the coast will be considered, in retrospect, a successful and enjoyable experience.

Chest waders are required from late fall through midspring. You should not skimp on cost when buying these items. Fishing during the above periods can be fun and very rewarding, but only if you are warm and dry. We buy our waders at Orvis. They are not inexpensive, but they are guaranteed, unless we rip them on barbed wire or a shell reef. We have had our waders replaced twice and repaired once at no cost to us. That sounds like a good deal to us. An associated piece of equipment is suspenders. We get ours at Orvis. They have been replaced once. Enough said.

Another important piece of equipment from the standpoint of personal comfort is a windbreaker/parka. Because of the cold-weather requirement for this piece of equipment, most anglers wear PVC raingear-type parkas. The most important characteristics of a good wadefishing parka are that it be waterproof and windproof, large enough to be worn over extra clothes and not restrict your movement, have non-corrosive zippers and snaps, an attached hood, and elastic at the wrists. The parka should be worn over the waders to prevent splash from entering your waders. Suggested colors include light green, blue or gray, or camouflage. Bright yellow may be fine in the boat, but while wading bright colors reflect off the water and spook fish.

Stringers should be 15 feet long. They should be made of stiffened $1/4$-inch nylon braided cord with a heavy stainless-steel needle on one end and a float on the other. The 20- to 25-foot models are intended for use where sharks are common. These long stringers are not intended to prevent sharks from hitting the fish while on your stringer. They are intended to carry your fish in such a way that a shark intent upon lunching on your speckled trout will not also, by accident, take a chunk out of your leg. Fish should be strung through the top lip and then the bottom lip. This allows them to swim upright and remain alive and fresh on the stringer for longer periods. Do not stringer fish through the gills, as this kills the fish quickly.

Another item that we would like to see in everyone's tackle box is called a Hookout. It is a tool designed to safely remove a barbed fishhook from a screaming person's body. We know that no one intends to have a hook buried in their arm, neck, shoulder, or anywhere else. We hope that none of us ever have to use this device, but if we do, it will be well worth the purchase price.

Pines Plaza Sporting Goods in Dickinson, Texas, has held a monthly big speckled trout contest since May 1983. The largest trout entered each month wins a prize. The name of each person weighing-in a speckled trout of 5-lb or more is entered into a monthly drawing for another prize. Pines Plaza's Mike Carlile has kept records on every speckled trout entered in his contest. All the fish were caught in the Galveston Bay system. The compiled statistics provide the most complete and accurate analysis of trophy speckled trout fishing available on the Texas Gulf Coast. Excerpts from this data will be included throughout this book:

- 90 percent of all entered speckled trout were caught using a popping rod measuring 7- to 7$^{1}/_{2}$-feet in length.
- 36 percent of the 5-lb + speckled trout were caught on 12-lb test line; 14-lb test line was second with 25 percent.
- 27 percent of the entered speckled trout were caught on Kelley-Wigglers; MirrOlure was second with 24 percent; live shrimp were third with 14 percent; Johnson Sprite spoon was fourth with 9 percent.
- LCI rods have consistently caught more entered fish than any other rod manufacturer. All Star is the second most popular.
- Shimano and Garcia are the most commonly used reels.
- Berkley Trilene XL-XT and DuPont Stren are the most popular lines used by the anglers entering fish in the contest.

These statistics are given to show successful trends. Some figures represent May 1983 through December 1988. Others represent shorter periods of time for which more complete data were available. All data are the property of and used by permission of Pines Plaza Sporting Goods, Mr. Mike Carlile, Dickinson, Texas. Go by and see them in Dickinson. You do not have to wait until you catch a 5-lb + speckled trout in Galveston.

FLY-FISHING EQUIPMENT

General Tackle

While proper selection of rod, reel, and line is important, the rod is by far the most critical part of the system for Texas bay fishing. The windy conditions generally found at the coast make moderate-to fast-action graphite rods a must. For redfish and speckled trout, an $8^1/2$- to $9^1/2$-foot rod for 6- to 10-weight lines can be used, depending on wind and the size and wind resistance of the flys being cast. The best bet for a beginning outfit is a 9-foot rod for an 8- or 9-weight line. Table 4 lists rods that are suitable for almost any bay fishing situation.

These rods range in price from $125 to $325. If you are new to saltwater fly-fishing, make an effort to cast several rods before you buy. And practice with your rod a little every day for a week or two before you head for the flats. A lesson from an experienced casting instructor can help you practice the right casting techniques.

You can choose your reel from a wide variety of saltwater models. There seem to be two or three new ones on the market every year. The five important features to look for are the type of drag system it employs, the materials from which it is made, whether it has a counter-balanced spool, whether the spool is exposed for palming, and to some extent, the reel's weight. You may be the proud owner of a beautiful (and expensive) classic trout reel, but if it isn't made of corrosion-resistant materials, you will rue the day you first exposed it to the brine.

While the more exotic saltwater species sought after by fly-fishermen, such as tarpon, bonefish, and permit, require huge line capacities

Table 4
Rods for Bay Fishing

Manufacturer	Model	Length (feet)	Line
J. Kennedy Fisher	Warm Water	9	8 or 9
G. Loomis	Premier	9	8
G. Loomis	1088 IM6	9	8
G. Loomis	1089 IMX	9	9
Orvis	9×9 Green Mountain	9	9
Orvis	9×9 XHLS 19	9	9
Sage	890RP	9	8 or 9
Sage	990 RPL	9	9

and high-tech drag systems, Texas bay species do not. With proper cleaning after each use, inexpensive reels, such as the Pfleuger Medalist, can give years of dependable service for less than $50. If you plan to try for the more exotic species sometime in the future, you should give consideration to some of the more sophisticated reels available on the market. These reels will run anywhere from $125 to $500 or more.

With a few exceptions, most of the upper Texas coastal bays are deeper than those found in Port O'Connor and further south. Galveston Bay, for example, is characterized by shorelines requiring fishermen to wade from knee- to chest-deep water.

A floating line will not allow the fly to get down to fish cruising near the bottom. The intermediate- (slow-) sinking line is perfect for this application because it allows you, by varying the density of your fly and the speed of your retrieve, to fish from the surface to a depth of about 4 feet. Conventional-sinking flylines sink faster at the thickest part of the taper, causing a bow in the flyline. The bow makes it more difficult for the angler to feel a soft strike and more difficult to set the hook. The new uniform sink-rate flyline from Scientific Angler sinks at the same rate throughout the taper, keeping the line straight during the retrieve. This is a major improvement in sinking-line construction. If you fish passes and deep channels, a super-fast sinking line is needed to get the fly down to where the fish are.

One additional note about leaders. The Orvis Company (and probably others as well) has developed a series of braided, tapered leaders. During the course of a day of fishing on the flats, you may need to change or replace a leader or tippet. In this event, you can struggle with any number of knots varying in complexity, or use a relatively new system of loop-to-loop connections. The Orvis braided leader allows for a much more flexible section from line to fly, thereby acting to significantly tighten the loop when casting. In the sometimes difficult-to-handle coastal winds on the Gulf Coast, a tight loop when casting can make quite a difference if your objective is to drop a shrimp-imitation 2 feet in front of a tailing redfish.

The best fly patterns for the upper coast include a wide variety of bait-fish imitations of Mullet patterns, such as Lefty's Deceivers #2-1/0 hooks, and #2-4 popping bugs, or Finger Mullet #1/0–3/0. We have absolutely nailed speckled trout and redfish with Orvis' Brown Snapping Shrimp #4 while fishing protected shoreline next to a stand of salt grass. Apparently, their Brown shrimp imitation does a fair job of imitating the real thing, which makes its home in the salt-grass marshes of the upper Texas Gulf Coast in late spring and early summer.

There are many other imitations that are effective up and down the Texas coast. Just like in the selection of any lure, the objective in selecting a fly should be to duplicate the size, action, and color of the bait upon which the fish are feeding. This decision, of course, cannot always be made until you are in the water. Most good fly-fishing shops can and do stock a supply of representative flies for their area. As you become more active as a fly-fisher, your assortment will grow beyond that which you can imagine.

One idea we find very helpful is to carry a separate box for each type of fly. When you arrive at an area to be fished, select several flys you feel will be most appropriate and put them in a smaller box that can be easily carried. As things tend to escape when carried on a wading belt or ditty bag, this idea can (and has for us) saved a considerable investment in flies on numerous occasions.

Consider as well the little extras found in most fly shops. We have no idea how some of these things are used, but some of them are indeed worth a second look. For instance, Orvis sells something called an "Improved Christmas Island Boot." This is a great boot for waders wherever they are. They provide protection against shells (and coral when fishing sub-equatorial environs) and are both durable and comfortable.

As the sport of fly-fishing grows on the Texas Gulf Coast, more and more people will discover just how effective this approach is for speckled trout and redfish. To get off to a good start, we wholeheartedly recommend contacting two friends of ours. They are Brooks Bouldin (713) 266-4493 and Dave Hayward (713) 783-2111. They do more than just sell equipment. They start slowly, and personally lead each customer through a process that results in equipment chosen for the right reasons and for the right type of fishing. They will then send you to one of many people they personally know on the Gulf Coast to teach you the art of fly-fishing.

CHAPTER 3

VARIABLES:
WHEN TO FISH

Each of us have thrown our hands up in the air and thought, or yelled, "Where are the fish?" In talking to hundreds of fishermen while selling our first book, a surprising truth became apparent to us. Many fishermen know three or four places to fish. Each time they go, they fish these same "secret spots." Sometimes they catch fish (at least once, or the spot would not have earned the "secret spot" status), and sometimes they do not. They have no idea why, in either case.

Our goal in writing this book is to teach the saltwater angler what factors impact his success ratio. What causes fish to feed and to be in a particular location at a particular time, and, more importantly, how to eliminate all of your unproductive "secret spots" and become more accurate in projecting when and where the fish will be. The basic factors affecting fish are the tides, the winds, and the water temperature. Combine these with the presence of bait fish in the water and you have something more like a 50/50 chance that fish will be there. That sounds like a whole lot better shot than sticking to "secret spots" and hoping that the fish come by.

TIDES

Tides are not understood by most people for one simple reason: They are very confusing! Because most fishermen are not astronomers (nor are we), and since a firm grasp of why tides do what they do is not necessary to understand how to use what they do to catch fish, our discussion will keep to the basics, the very basics.

Tides are affected by the relative positions of the sun, the moon, and the earth, and the gravitational pulls exerted on the earth by the sun and the moon. The moon's effect is more pronounced because we are closer to the moon than the sun. Tides occur at different times of the day because the lunar day is shorter than the solar day of 24 hours. When the sun and moon are directly aligned (full and new moons) their combined gravitational fields cause higher-than-normal tides. These are called spring tides (not related to the season before summer). When the sun and moon exert their gravitational forces at right angles to each other (first and third quarter moons), lower than usual tides occur. These are called neap tides.

The reference point for Texas coastal tides is the foot of 20th Street on the Galveston Ship Channel. This point was selected by the National Ocean Service, not the Galveston Chamber of Commerce. The National Oceanic and Atmospheric Administration publications, which cover the entire world, list 27 correction points for Texas. These publications may be purchased from the National Ocean Service, Riverdale, Maryland 20737-1199, or from a government bookstore or a marine store. The applicable correction points for this book are listed in the Appendix under "Tidal Differences Chart." These differences can be significant. Factors contributing to these are the size and shape of the bay and its location within its bay system, and its number and size of links to the Gulf.

Winds also affect tides. Wind, however, only affects the amplitude of the tide, not its time. A strong easterly wind will hold water in the bays, increasing the amplitude of the high and decreasing the effect of the low tide. Westerly winds have the opposite effect, causing lower high and low tides. A strong north wind will also tend to blow water out of the bays. Rivers flowing into the bays also affect tide amplitude. River inflow will impede an incoming (flood) tide and enhance an outgoing (ebb) tide.

Just a few more quick definitions for you to try on your friends: high tide or stand—highest level reached by an incoming tide; low tide or stand—lowest level reached; diurnal tides—one high and one low tide occurring in one day; semidiurnal—you guessed it, two highs and two lows in one day; slack water—a period of no tidal flow not to be confused with the stand, which is when the vertical rise or fall stops.

Tidal movement increases feeding activity. Your location within the bay system dictates which tides are best and how you should fish during each. Many anglers believe that four tides a day provide better fishing than two tidal changes. If you are in a bay close to the pass(es) which link it to the Gulf, then we concur. If, however, you are in a bay whose tidal correction time is 4 or 5 hours from that of the base point, the movement of the tides may be significantly reduced by the time it gets there, yielding long periods of slack water. This is true because of the smaller amplitudes of change typically found in semidiurnal tides. Conversely, diurnal tides with their increased amplitude and extended periods of movement may be more productive in the more removed areas.

All tides are not created equal. The important number in a tide chart is not the time, but the amplitude, or height of the stand, and this number should be compared to the stand of the previous tide to determine how much water is actually going to move. The change from a low to a high could be as little as 1.2 inches in 3 hours or as much or more than 25 inches over a 16 hour period. Actual tidal movement can begin 4 or 5 hours or more before the time indicated for the stand or very close to the time, dependent upon amplitude and the wind. Tide changes are very important in that changes in their environment cause changes in the fish's activity. Fishing around passes can be most productive during the first 2 hours after the tide changes direction. The same is true for the mouths of bayous and canals as the tide starts to fall from a high stand. For an incoming tide, we prefer to be there the whole time it is rising; however, many prefer the 2 hours before and the 2 hours after high stand. The time for high stand is, of course, the time published in the tide chart.

The direction of the tidal movement affects the fish relative to their surrounding environment. In shallow bays, the fish use guts as ambush points in which to intercept bait moving with the tide. The same holds true for passes. An incoming tide will flood the ditches, coves, bayous, salt-grass marshes, and flats with food. An outgoing tide will drain these and the resident marine life out of these same areas or concentrate them in the deepest portions of the area. On an incoming tide, work the guts, flats, shorelines, and into the marshes for foraging fish. As the tide starts to recede, shift your attention to the mouths of these tributaries. The fish will gather there, to dine on the food washed out of the marshes that serve as the bay system's nursery grounds for all kinds of marine life, and also in the guts leading to deeper water and the potholes themselves.

Reefs also serve as buffet tables for predators. Redfish scour the reefs, rooting around looking for shrimp, crabs, and anything else small enough to fit into their mouths. Speckled trout tend to gather on the downcurrent side of the reef and wait for the tide to bring shrimp and bait fish to them. They are much more delicate than redfish and do not, therefore, browse in the shell itself. Speckled trout like reefs because the shrimp can not bury themselves in the mud when the speckled trout arrive, as they can elsewhere with a soft bottom. The same holds true for the oyster-shell pads laid as a base for drilling and production platforms.

Tides are the most important factor in planning where to and when to fish. An understanding of these will go a long way toward making you a more consistently successful fisherman. Finally, we offer you a tidbit from the 1988 edition of Pines Plaza Sporting Goods' monthly speckled trout tournament: Eight of the twelve monthly winners were caught within three days on either side of a full or new moon. So, do not forget that spring tides can mean trophy fish.

WINDS

Winds affect both the fish and the fisherman greatly. Wind determines the clarity of the water and this, in turn, dictates how and where the fisherman will fish and, in some instances, where the fish will be. Speckled trout are sight feeders. While they are feeding, if they see something that appears to be alive and it is smaller than they are, they will eat it. To the fisherman, this not-too-exaggerated statement means that their bait or lure must appear alive and be visible to the speckled trout in order to catch them with any consistency. Redfish, on the other hand, are scent feeders. They love to root around on their noses in mud and shell, scrounging up crabs and shrimp. However, they also catch and eat mullet and other finfish. They do not do this with their noses. For lures to be effective, there must be 18 inches of visibility through the water. With less than that, use live bait. Both species can smell live bait in the water; however, speckled trout will move to find clear water on the upper coast. On the lower coast, with clear water everywhere, speckled trout will look for off-color water in which to hide from their prey. Off-color water on the lower coast is frequently trout-green water on the upper coast. That is correct: Lower coast anglers look for "off-color" water and upper coast anglers look for clear water. Clear and off-color are relative terms, and in this particular instance, may offer a similar visibility.

Southeast wind at less than 10 knots is the ideal on the Texas coast. This clears the surf and allows the incoming tides to clear the bays. The worst wind for fishing the coast is a southwest wind. Even a light southwest wind will cloud the surf and turn the bays sandy. A southwest wind of any duration will reduce the water to the color of chocolate milk, with a similar visibility. Any wind over 15 knots will make fishing uncomfortable, at best, and potentially dangerous. Fishing the leeward, or protected shorelines, is called for in these instances. Land will, at least partially, block the wind, and it prevents the wind from clouding up the water. Trout will seek out these clear pockets in search of food. Therefore, wind direction should be an important aspect in planning each trip to the coast. Fish areas protected from the wind. Wading protected shorelines from the shore is an alternative to staying home and pouting when small craft advisories persuade you not to drag your boat to the coast.

Easterly winds hold water in the bay, increasing the high tide and decreasing the effect of the low tide. Westerly winds have the opposite effect, creating lower high and low tides. These factors should be considered when planning where to fish, as well as where to launch and recover the boat.

WATER TEMPERATURE

As with salinity and water clarity, speckled trout are more sensitive to water temperature than are redfish. Speckled trout will be found where the water temperature is within their preferred levels.

In the spring, usually in April, as the beachwater temperature breaks and maintains the 70° mark, speckled trout fishing becomes a more consistent pursuit. Beachwater temperatures near 65° will put the water temperature on the flats near 70°. There can be 3° to 7° difference between the water temperature on the flats and the beach.

In the spring migration, the big speckled trout appear in the bays first. These fish will feed on the shorelines until the water temperature exceeds 83°, usually in early July. At this time, they will seek the cooler water of the deep reefs and well pads during the days, and venture onto the shorelines only during the cool of the night and early mornings. Bright sun again forces the fish to deep water. This pattern will hold until fall, when the beachwater temperature falls below 80°. The trout then return to the shorelines. They will continue to feed on the shorelines until the water temperature drops below 55°. At that time they again go to deep water, to the deepest holes they can find, to take advantage of the warm water found there.

Knowing how water temperature affects the fish you seek will enable you to increase your effectiveness on the water. It is one more piece of the trip-planning puzzle.

CHAPTER 4

AREA SUMMARIES: WHERE TO FISH

EAST TEXAS AREA

Sabine Lake

Location: Sabine Lake is due east of Port Arthur on the Texas/Louisiana border in southeast Texas.

Access: Texas Highway 87 parallels the eastern shore of Sabine Lake, but access to most points at the south end of the lake and Sabine Pass are reached from Texas Highway 82. To reach Texas Highway 82, cross the Intracoastal Waterway to Pleasure Island by using the Martin Luther King bridge. This highway then goes south to the causeway at the south end of the lake and on across to Louisiana. To fish the north end of the lake, go north on Texas Highway 87 past Rainbow Bridge. Turn right at the first road. This will take you to Rob Bailey's Bait Camp on Old River Cove. For access to the middle of the lake, launch at the public ramp on Pleasure Island. The Tackle Box, which is near the ramp, should have any last-minute item you need for your trip. If you are going to fish the south end of the lake, you can launch at the causeway bridge at state ramps on either side of the Texas/Louisiana border. Even though you can reach the jetties from these ramps on the causeway, you can reduce your running time by launching at a ramp

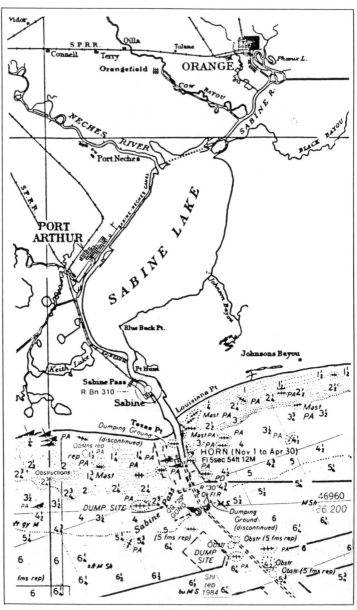

EAST TEXAS AREA

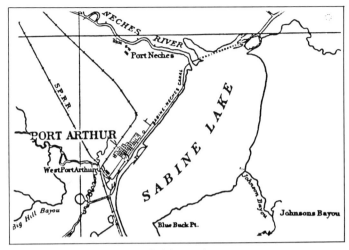

Sabine Lake

in the Township of Sabine Pass off Texas Highway 87. This makes sense, especially if you are going to be there all day.

Bottom conditions: Hard and soft sand throughout the lake, with areas of significant oyster shell reefs; some mud near the eastern shore and in the bayous.

Special equipment: Boat. The vast majority of hot spots we recommend are fished by boat.

When and Where: Before we turn you loose on the lake, we need to make you aware of a unique regulations problem. Sabine Lake is a border lake, and each state bordering the lake has its own game laws. Texas requires fisherman to hold a valid fishing license and own a current state saltwater stamp. To fish the Louisiana side of the lake, you must hold a valid non-resident fishing license (assuming you are not a Louisiana resident) and a valid saltwater license. All of these are available on both sides of the lake. Remember that size and number limits differ. To be on the safe side, Texas fishermen should have all the documents mentioned above, and then live within the quotas established by Texas law.

The Louisiana shore borders the Sabine National Wildlife Refuge. This refuge provides a tremendous estuary for all kinds of critters, and a haven for wadefishermen. The area from the Johnson Bayous to Whiskey Bayou is a great place to start. The bottom there is soft sand and clam shells and generally holds tailing redfish close to shore. Fish the mouth of any bayou and remember the area is also loaded with flounder. Our lures of choice are a gold spoon or white and pink curly-tail grubs. Next, try Coffee Ground Cove. You will find a bottom of hard sand and oyster reefs that provide the best wadefishing area for speckled trout. Use gold or silver spoons or live shrimp under a popping cork.

Our next recommendation is not in Sabine Lake at all. It is, however, in the area and almost every wadefisherman we know puts it on his list of hot spots in the dog days of summer, particularly July. Access to this area is off Texas Highway 87 just west of Sabine Pass. Go to McFadden Beach and fish Mud Flats. Look for two things: green water, and shad or pogies being driven to the surface. Several locals we know use a 1/2-oz Pro-Trap. It's a real killer for big trout cruising the surf. Another good bait is a 52MR series MirrOlure, preferably an 11, 26, or 704. When the artificials quit producing, use your cast net and go after those shad. Fish these under a popping cork; you will find them to be excellent for big trout.

Back in the lake, start on the Louisiana side of the causeway and wade to Blue Buck Point. Use 51MR, 26, or 52MR11 MirrOlures or strawberry (or smoke in the spring) shrimptails with 1/4-oz jig heads. The last recommended hot spot for waders is the southwest corner of the lake starting at the point where the western bank begins to head north. Fish back toward Mesquite Point with shrimptail jigs (particularly white, pearl, or chartreuse), gold spoons, or live shrimp under a popping cork.

Drifting is another story. For fishing the south end of the lake, launch at the causeway bridge. Head north about 1,000 yards and drift numerous oyster-shell reefs in 4 to 10 feet of water. This area can be a producer anytime, but is best on an incoming tide from November through April. Local guide Jerry Norris recommends jig heads with red, black, or purple Shad Gilraker worms.

In the spring, as shrimp begin their annual migration to the Gulf from Sabine Lake, fish the birds. They are always effective fish locators and rarely lie. As word gets out in Seagulldom that shrimp have been spotted, the birds become greedy and all too emotional. Their excitement can be heard and seen for miles. Look first, of course, for a hovering or excited bird carefully eyeing a point on the water where nothing seems to be happening. What has probably happened is a shrimp or other acceptable bait fish has been driven to the surface in order that it might escape a predator below, only to find aerial reinforcements providing a threat above. Multiply that single shrimp by ten thousand and the predator by several hundred and you can understand why, for the birds, this can truly be a beak-licking experience. You will also find that most of this commotion occurs when the shrimp have been driven over or to an oyster reef where escape to a soft bottom is virtually eliminated. Often, after the storm subsides and the fan has been cleaned, specks may still remain. Unless you can see a repeat performance nearby, drift the area again.

The north end of the lake should be fished out of Rob Bailey's Bait Camp on Old River Cove. Just outside the mouth of the cove you will cross the Sabine-Neches Canal. There you will find three islands on the lake side of the canal. On the canal side of these islands you will find a significant drop-off. This change in depth and the resulting change in temperature can produce great results, as the flats become too warm in the summer. Also, remember redfish thrive in the brackish water created by runoff from the Neches and Sabine rivers. On the south (or lake side of these islands) you will find considerable structure. As we all know, speed in shallow water and underwater obstructions tend to provide countless new ways of re-distributing the bottom of your boat to an area noticeably larger than it occupied when originally designed. So, be careful!

The area south of these islands, particularly Stewts and Sidney Islands, is fairly firm and supports several oyster reefs. Combined with other structures, it provides an excellent area to drift for speckled trout. At this same end of the lake you will notice several production platforms due south of West Pass. These platforms tend to hold speckled trout, and are worth trying with live bait under a popping cork, or with a strawberry shrimptail jig. This can be done by drifting the area or from an anchored boat.

The last recommended area to drift is Coffee Ground Flats. You should be in about 5 feet of water fishing over hard sand and oyster

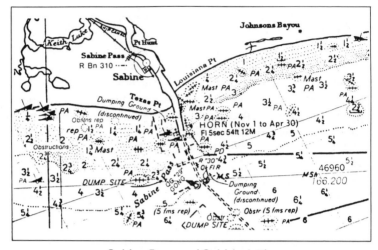

Sabine Pass and Sabine Jetties

shell. Live shrimp under a popping cork, shrimptail jigs (strawberry), or white and pink curly-tail grubs are our choice. As you drift near the shore, keep an eye out for any action in the water. A long drift can very quietly put you on top of unsuspecting fish working the flats. And it just so happens these flats are fed by the very productive Sabine National Wildlife Refuge.

Sabine Pass and Sabine Jetties

For purposes of this discussion, we will not recommend the Pass itself for speckled trout and redfish. We know they are caught there, but our experience has been that there are several locations in the area that provide better opportunities. In the fall, however, the Pass can be a hot spot for flounder and other species heading to the Gulf.

The Sabine Jetties are fished almost entirely by boat and on the Texas side. When green water shows up at the Sabine Jetties, so do the fishermen. There is no consensus of opinion as to which bait is best, although live shrimp and croaker fished at or near the bottom are recommended by trophy hunters.

GALVESTON AREA

Rollover Pass

Location: From Galveston, take the free ferry from the east end of Galveston Island across Bolivar Roads to the Bolivar Peninsula. As you leave the ferry, you will be on Texas 87. Rollover Fish Pass (its real name) is 20 miles up the Bolivar Peninsula at Gilchrist. Coming from Houston or Beaumont, take IH 10 to the Winnie exit, Texas 124. Take this road to the coast at High Island, turn right and go 8 miles. Rollover Pass is a manmade link between the back of East Bay and the Gulf. It was built to help regulate the salinity of the back portion of East Bay, at a location used by smugglers to roll contraband brought in from the Gulf to waiting boats in East Bay, thus the name Rollover Pass.

Access: Wadefishing is done on both the east and west sides of the Gulf side of the Pass. Wading the bay side of the Pass is done (usually for flounder), but is difficult because of the soft mud bottom. Fishing from the bulkhead is also popular, with most speckled trout and redfish caught from the east Gulf side.

Services: Numerous bait/tackle shops and snack bars are located at the Pass. A public boat ramp on the Intracoastal Canal is located 1/4 mile from the Pass on Yacht Basin Road (no yacht basin or anything resembling one is there, however) behind the Gilchrist Western Auto. This does not provide boat access to the Pass. Boat traffic is prohibited in Rollover Pass.

Special Equipment: Life preserver.

When and Where: Rollover Pass is fished by two types of fisherman: the long rod, pyramid sinker, lawnchair variety, and the if-fish-are-there-so-am-I type of wadefisherman. The latter is easily recognized because they are wet from head to toe, have red eyes from the salt and sun, throw only hardware, carry fish on stringers instead of chunking them in the cooler in their vehicle, and usually have more fish than their more sedentary counterparts. To say Rollover exacts a price from these anglers for their fish is an obvious understatement. Waves breaking over your head and floating with the swells are

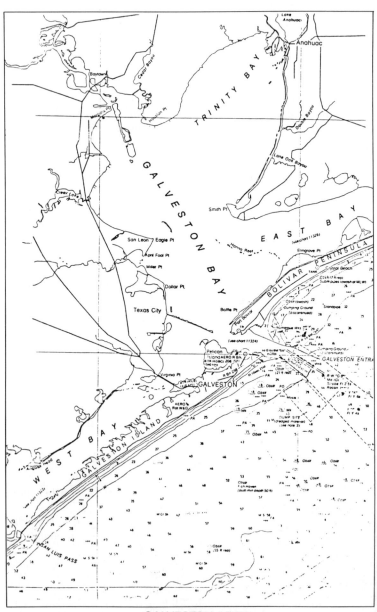

GALVESTON AREA

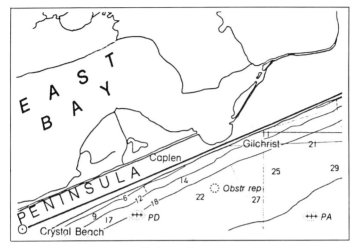

Rollover Pass

commonplace, but so are limits of speckled trout, which explains it to all of us who love those snaggle-tooth freckled-face fellas.

Rollover Pass is a consistent producer of speckled trout and occasional redfish from May through July, when the water heats up, and again in late September through October, as the water cools. Waders are obviously not worn at Rollover as to do so would be asking to be drowned. Wet suits are worn by those veterans who chase the fish in the spring and fall, while those of us without such equipment just get cold. The coldest we have ever been while fishing was when it was 71° outside, 71° in the water, and a very brisk wind was blowing under overcast skies . . . but we were catching speckled trout! You can always get warm after the fish quit biting.

An outgoing (ebb) tide is required to catch fish at Rollover on the Gulf side. The best time is right after the change from slack to outgoing. Usually, the fish show up as the tide begins to pick up some momentum; however, they are occasionally there as it starts and gone by the time it picks up any speed. The east Gulf side is favored by the artificial-lure fisherman. A pilgrim on that side with shrimp and a cork will incur the wrath of everyone present. Fishing the two side-by-side in the current is impossible. Live-bait fisherman should use the west Gulf side.

Water depth at the mouth of the pass varies from year to year, and sometimes from month to month. Some years you can walk out to the end of the pilings comfortably and sometimes you have to swim, depending upon where Mother Nature has moved the sand bars. Likewise, beyond the pilings, you may have an area of 50 yards or so to fish parallel to the pass, or you may only have 50 feet before the water is up to your neck. The current in the pass can be treacherous. You can not afford to become so involved in changing lures or untying tangles that you forget to monitor your location in relationship to the fast water and the drop-off. It can easily happen. That is why you should always have a life preserver with you, even if you do not have it on.

When the fish are there, so are the fisherman. At this location, almost everyone will be using similar, if not identical, lures. You will be almost shoulder to shoulder with other fisherman each of whom will be throwing into the current and retrieving. Everyone casts in front of them and at about the same distance, and retrieves at about the same speed. It only takes one bozo who cannot make his equipment work to turn the scene into a disaster of 5 or 6 tangled lines. This does not make the regulars happy. Know what you are doing and continually be aware of the others around you, and you will have a much better trip to Rollover.

Hot lures for Rollover change. One of the most consistent, and hardest to find, is the Porter Seahawk. Another version of this lure is called the Coast Hawk. It is a short, heavy lure with two treble hooks that is an absolute killer in the current at Rollover. Colors do not seem to be critical with this lure. We prefer red/white, red/yellow, and blue/yellow. The next best producers are the MirrOlures (51, 52, 60, and 65 series). Most popular are the 28, 11, 12, 12FGO, 54, 801, 21, and 751. KelleyWigglers, $1/2$- and $3/4$-ozRattletraps in chrome painted like a 28, TT28, 11, and TT11 MirrOlures, and spoons in $3/4$- and $11/4$-oz (gold and silver) are also proven lures. It is necessary to carry extra lures with you while at Rollover. An underwater obstruction commonly referred to as "the cable" (more commonly referred to as the "expletive deleted" cable), runs from the mouth of the pass out for about 20 or 30 feet. Connection with this monster usually results in having to break your line, done quickly to avoid having all lures cast upstream tangling on your stationary line, and retie. This is particularly distressing when the offending lure was the last of the only model that is catching fish that day.

The veteran bulkhead anglers use heavier rods and fish the bottom using fish-finder rigs with 2-foot-long leaders below a 4-oz pyramid weight. They use live mullet or shad (menhaden) that they catch in a cast net and keep alive in an aerated cooler. They prefer the Gulf end of the east side of the Pass and cast into the middle of the Pass. Their weight will roll in the current on the sandbar running down the middle of the Pass until it falls off the bar into the gut on either side of the bar or one of several holes washed out by the current. Look for the gaps in the wall going out into the Gulf to locate these holes. They place their rods in rod holders made of 18 inches of 2-inch diameter PVC pipe which they sink into the shell next to the bulkhead. This is easily done by cutting the bottom of the rod holder into two points and twisting it into the shell. The bases of the retaining wall are full of lost line, remnants of lost cast nets, and all means of miscellaneous sea junk. To allow your line to get into close proximity to this is to loose it. Fish are landed from the bulkhead with long nets. The net with a 6-foot handle that telescopes to 12-feet is a favorite. Attempting to land a large fish without such a net (yours or one you borrowed from a neighbor) usually results in a lost fish. Plan ahead.

Rollover Pass is a popular stop for all types of fish and fisherman. Knowing what you are doing will make it an enjoyable experience.

East Bay

Location: East Bay is located north of Bolivar Peninsula and south of Smith Point.

Access: Public access to East Bay is almost exclusively limited to boaters. The reasons for this are: (1) the Intracoastal Waterway cuts through the Bolivar Peninsula denying land access from it to East Bay's south shoreline, and (2) the north shoreline is almost all private land. Public access is available in two places, the Anahuac National Wildlife Refuge and Smith Point. The primary road is FM 1985, running from Texas 124 on the east to where FM 562 branches off and leads to Smith Point. Only a few of the access roads from FM 1985 and FM 562 are available for public access. For the boater access is unlimited, only a

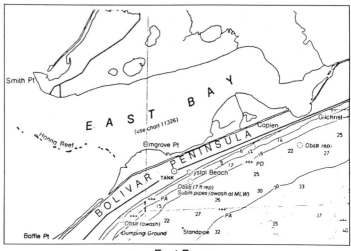

East Bay

short run from the Texas City Dike, Eagle Point, the Galveston Yacht Basin, and any of several marinas on the Bolivar Peninsula.

Services: Any of the above locations can provide bait, tackle, and fisherman's groceries.

Special Equipment: Boat.

When and Where: East Bay is one of the smaller bays in the Galveston system, but has several factors that ensure that it will consistently be a top producer of speckled trout and redfish. Some of these contributors are its miles of untouched salt-grass marshes, its relatively constant salinity, and its abundance of natural and manmade structure. Its marshes have been spared from the assault of "progress" for primarily two reasons. The marshes on the southern side of the Bay are buffered from commercialization by the Intracoastal Waterway, which runs through the Bolivar Peninsula. The northern marshes are protected by large, stable estates, whose owners choose not to develop the land, or because they are a portion of the Anahuac National Wildlife Refuge and as such are protected by law. The constant salinity is attributable to the Bay's two links to the Gulf. To the west, East Bay adjoins Lower Galveston Bay, less than 5 miles from the open Gulf through the

Galveston Jetties. To the east, Rollover Fish Pass provides a manmade link to the Gulf built solely to provide access to the Gulf from East Bay for the fish while circulating water to maintain uniform saline levels in East Bay.

The natural structure of East Bay is an abundance of oyster reefs. The manmade structures are the shell pads laid to support petroleum drilling platforms. Some are visible from existing above-surface structure, others are unmarked on the surface; however, both serve as artificial reefs and will, at times, hold fish. Another attribute of East Bay is its lack of heavy industrial and commercial boat traffic, all of which is routed through the Intracoastal Waterway and Lower Galveston Bay, except during oyster season, which is November through the following April.

Fishing East Bay begins in the spring. Winter is usually sandy and rough, courtesy of the season's northers. As the spring sun warms the beachfront, water temperatures climb past 65° and move toward 70°, and southerly and southeasterly winds clear the water, the fish hit the shorelines. Fishing is accomplished by either wading or drifting the shorelines. Which shoreline is determined by wind direction. North to northeast winds; wade the north shoreline. South to southeast winds; wade the south shoreline. Favorite spring wading locations on the south shoreline include Fat Rat Pass, Elmgrove Point, Pepper Point, and Baffle Point to Hannas Reef. Additional south shoreline favorites include the area from Fat Rat Pass to Long Point, with emphasis around Stingaree Cut. A quick check on a map will show that we have selected almost the entire south shoreline as prime spring wading territory. In this area, as summer winds wipe out the Bolivar Wells or Hannas Reef, try wading at first light east of Pepper Point near Hannas. In the spring, the north shoreline from the beach at the Anahuac NWR (Frozen Point) to Smith Point can be good. Summer usually means that the western half is more productive, from Stephenson Point to Smith Point.

As the water temperature maintains and passes the 75° mark, the fish are found on the reefs as well as near the shorelines. Hannas Reef is the most famous reef in the Galveston complex. It is crescent shaped and stretches from Pepper Point on the south shoreline almost to Smith Point. It comprises 1,300 acres of shell reef, some of which is alive, with two passes—Ladies Pass and Moodys Cut—cut through it. Both of these are excellent locations for speckled trout and redfish.

Deep Reef and the smaller scattered patches of shell are also excellent producers. They are generally midbay, north of Elmgrove Point southeast toward Hannas Reef. This shell gets little publicity in the summer, with those fishermen usually attributing their success to a nebulous area "near Hannas." (It is similar to the immense area attributed to "around Greens Cut" in West Bay during the winter). The point east of Hannas is productive and usually far less crowded. Other productive reefs are Frenchy's, east of Deep and west of Long Point in 3 to 4 feet of water, and the Pepper Grove Reefs between Elmgrove Point and Fat Rat Pass. These are also shallow, but their deep sides are in 5 to 6 feet of water.

In late June and July, the East Bay fishing centers on the Bolivar Wells, or rather the shell pads laid to support the drilling platforms there. The wells, composed of approximately 50 shell pads of which perhaps half have structure above the water, sit in 8 to 25 feet of water. The pads are from 3 to 10 feet thick. An electronic depth finder is the key to finding the unmarked pads. The key to the pads is gently moving water. The current will dictate which pads will hold fish. The stronger the current, the further you should move away from the channel. If the current is weaker, move closer. The pros prefer to fish the Wells before a tide change, just prior to it starting or stopping its movement. Green water is a must at the Wells. Because of the Wells' location, a single green tide can clear them out, where it may take two or three green tides to clear out East Bay.

Another time to head to East Bay is when Trinity Bay, its neighbor to the north, has runoff problems, either too much or too little. When Trinity Bay becomes too salty (too little runoff from its tributaries) or too fresh or "sweet," (too much rain to the north swelling the rivers and dumping into Trinity Bay), the speckled trout move to the saltier water, right into East Bay. At times the freshwater/saltwater line can be seen. If you find it, you will find speckled trout stacked up against it. Remember, Trinity Bay's problems can equate to limits of fish to the East Bay angler who takes advantage of nature's concentrating the fish into one bay.

East Bay anglers use artificials, KelleyWigglers, MirrOlures, spoons, and Redfins on the shorelines, as well as shrimp under popping corks. Reef fisherman do the same. At the Wells, KelleyWigglers or live shrimp near the bottom on a fish-finder rig are the norm. East Bay is

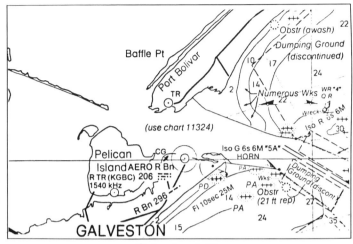

Galveston Jetties

hot from spring through late fall. To close, a couple of facts from Pines Plaza Sporting Goods' monthly speckled trout contests:

- 54 percent of the 9-lb + speckled trout that have won the monthly tournament since it began came from East Bay. Trinity and West Bay tied for second with 15 percent.
- 25 percent of all monthly winners came from East Bay, second only to West Bay with 34 percent.

Galveston Jetties

Location: The North Jetty reaches 6.3 miles into the Gulf from the southeast end of Bolivar Peninsula, while the south reaches 5.4 miles from the northeast end of Galveston Island, forming the largest jetty complex on the west coast of the Gulf of Mexico. The North Jetty is about 2 miles from the ferry landing at Bolivar on Texas 87. There is a large bait-camp sign with an arrow directing where to turn right to drive to the base of the North Jetty. Parking is limited due to the number of bait camps and beer joints located on this road. For the South Jetty, take Seawall Boulevard to the northeast end of Galveston Island. As Seawall Boulevard dead-ends into the water, turn right and follow the road to Apfel Park. During the summer, you will be charged a parking fee to enter the Park. The South Jetty is at the far end of the park. Parking is not usually a problem on the open beach.

Access: The North Jetty is flat-topped for almost 3/4 mile. Rock walkers can walk out to the Boat Cut, which is about another 1/2 mile after the flat-top stops. The South Jetty begins at the Coast Guard Station with its next 3.4 miles wrapped around the end of Galveston Island. Approximately 2 miles of South Jetty extends into the Gulf. The first 1/2 mile is flat-topped, but has several areas where waves wash across low spots in the rocks, creating a semi-hazardous crossing to all but the most sure-footed and light-traveling rock walkers. It is possible to walk almost all the way to the old abandoned South Jetty Lighthouse, approximately 1/4 mile from the seaward end of the Jetty.

Services: Boaters have, of course, excellent access to both jetties, with launching available on the South Jetty (these can be tricky in low-tide conditions), the Galveston Yacht Basin, and the Texas City Dike, plus several marinas on the Bolivar Peninsula.

Special Equipment: None.

When and Where: North Jetty—Water depth on the channel side extends from a few feet (in mud) near the shoreline to 20 feet at the Small Boat Cut (its real name), and then 30 feet to about half the remaining length of the Jetty; from there it hits 40 feet as far away as 300 yards from the Outer Bar Channel. On the Gulf side, wading is possible almost out to where the flat-top stops. The depth increases from the Boat Cut to 30 feet near its seaward end. There is a 52-foot-deep hole 100 yards in diameter off the end of the Jetty. The Tower Hole is on the Gulf side 150 yards inside of the Boat Cut. The Washboard Rock Hole is on the Gulf side at the second dogleg, 300 yards from the large sunken ship. On the channel side, there is a hole 100 yards inside the Boat Cut. The Coffin Hole is where the Jetty makes the big dogleg and the Cobia Hole is 100 yards from the end.

The Tower Hole is a stretch of the Jetty that produces excellent speckled trout fishing in late spring and early summer. Washboard Rock Hole also produces well in late spring and early summer. From here to almost the end of the Jetty offers excellent fishing. The Sunken Ship provides excellent fishing for large redfish in March. These waters extending a mile from the Jetty, are the location of numerous sunken ships. In the summer, fish congregate around these wrecks and are easy prey to the knowledgeable angler. Coffin and Cobia are best at the change of a high tide and through the first 2 hours of the outgoing tide. Speckled trout are most abundant from the middle of May through August, using shrimp under a popping cork or shrimp on the bottom using enough weight on a fish-finder rig to keep your bait near the bottom. September is a hot month for redfish. (Flounder are everywhere, 200 yards on either side of the Boat Cut on the channel side during the fall.)

South Jetty—Most rock walkers fish the Gulf side. A huge sand bar, Big Reef, on the channel side extends approximately halfway to the end of the Jetty. Except where the sand bar is, the channel-side depths range from 21 feet at the Coast Guard Station to 30 feet at the end. The Gulf side varies from a few feet at the base to 30 feet at the end. Immediately off the end is a 41-foot hole. About 100 yards from the end of the Jetty on the channel side is a 57-foot hole, called Redfish Hole. Pointed Rock Hole is on the channel side between the Lighthouse and the end, measuring 36-feet-deep.

Pointed Rock is best known for redfish, legal and oversized, as is Redfish Hole. The Gulf side, from halfway out to the end, is best for speckled trout, using shrimp under a popping cork or artificials. Fleenor's Flats, on the channel side, is located between channel marker 11 and the Jetty. A depth finder is required to find it. Its depth goes from 30 feet to 10 feet. Leaving the Flats toward the Jetty, the depth drops to 20 feet. The Flats are best known for bull reds in the fall. The pocket between the South Jetty and the Gulf can also provide excellent big speckled trout fishing in the winter. The mouth of the Lagoon, to your right as you go toward Apfel Park from the Seawall, can also provide big speckled trout in April and May on outgoing tides.

Most fishing at the Jetties is done at anchor. The best approach is to anchor close to the rocks. The fish may be near the visible rocks or they may be 30 or 40 yards from the Jetties. The base of the Jetties are much wider than the visible portion of the rocks. Positioning in this manner will allow you to fish both areas. Depth finders are extremely important around the Jetties. These provide the angler with the capability of finding small holes and large boulders that are separated from the main body of rocks. These small irregularities can hold 1 to 3 fish at any time. The ability to take advantage of these anomalies can sometimes mean the difference between a successful and a semi-successful or mediocre jetty experience.

Moving water is critical at the Jetties. The basic rules are to fish the Gulf channel side on an incoming tide, and to fish the channel side between the Jetties on an outgoing tide. Winds are also critical. Use the wind to determine which Jetty to fish. Fish the protected side of the Jetty that will put you into the correct tidal movement. Strong east winds blow "down the rocks," and discolor the water, making fishing unproductive and uncomfortable. West winds are absolutely the worst throughout the coast. Northerly and southerly components will dictate your location. Another rule involves presentation. It is best to drift your bait through the target area as opposed to fishing it stationary in the area. Sometimes, however, this is easier said than done.

Bolivar Pocket—Access to the Bolivar Pocket is from the eastern side of Loop 108, approximately 4 miles from the ferry landing on Texas 87. Turn right toward the beach and then right again at the beach. Drive until you reach the barricades that keep you out of a bird sanctuary at the end of the Peninsula. Wading is usually done out from where you park and then back toward the North Jetty. Use artificials, MirrOlures, KelleyWigglers, and spoons through mid-July. From then through September, use shrimp under a popping cork. Much has been written about the sharks (yes, sharks) in the Pocket, and how no one takes live bait there. We do, and we do so for one reason—to catch fish. When the water is 85° +, it takes shrimp to catch fish. We have never caught or seen a shark, nor have we ever seen or heard of a stringer being hit by a shark while we were there. That is not to say that it does not or will not happen, but we have spent considerable time there with and without shrimp, and it has not happened yet.

We fish the Bolivar Pocket during incoming tides, particularly in southwest winds. The North Jetty allows this area to maintain clear water longer than anywhere else in the bays. Start fishing when you are in knee-deep water. The fish are frequently in the first gut. We catch mostly speckled trout and flounder there, along with an occasional redfish. The bottom is hard sand, with the usual mud in the guts. If you are using bait, fish around others using bait. The combination of all that bait in the water can attract and hold fish in the area. Conversely, if using hardware, stay away from the bait fisherman.

Bolivar Flats—Access to the Bolivar Flats is from Texas 87 approximately 1/2 mile from the ferry landing. Park your vehicle on the side of the road and wade. We have been most successful fishing the drop-off adjacent to Fort Travis. This area is best during incoming tides with green water.

Fort Travis—This is deep water and can be fished by boat or from the rocks, no wading. Again, look for incoming tides and green water. The deeper water will hold fish when the adjacent flats are too hot to suit speckled trout. Use shrimp under a popping cork.

The Galveston Jetties are excellent from May through October. They provide many different types of structures and habitats for fish. Match the conditions to the location and you are in for a very enjoyable experience.

Trinity Bay

Location: Trinity Bay is the largest and northernmost bay in the Galveston complex. It is north of Smith Point and joins Upper Galveston Bay from the northeast.

Access: Trinity Bay is almost exclusively the domain of the boaters. Launching facilities are located at Baytown, Anahuac, Double Bayou, and Smith Point. Boats may also launch from Eagle Point and the various Bolivar marinas. Launch locations should be dictated by the weather and the intended fishing location. Land access to Trinity Bay is limited at best. Boatless waders may gain access along the Tri-city Beach Road, at McCullum Park, and at Smith Point. The Complete Angler, a marina at Smith Point, rents boats with motors and provides a wader's shuttle service, primarily to the Vingt-Et-Un Island area. Check with the Complete Angler for details.

Services: Minimal.

Special Equipment: Boat.

When and Where: Trinity Bay offers the inshore angler all the available options to catch fish almost year round. It has miles of hard-sand shorelines with shell reefs, spoil islands, and a long eastern shoreline to block the predominant southeast wind. For the boat-bound fisherman, it offers both shallow and deep reefs, a lot of 9- to 10-foot

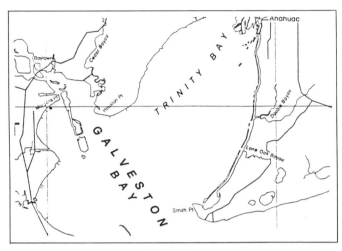

Trinity Bay

water, and many gas wells and drilling platforms above the surface to help anglers find their shell pads and "secret" pads with no surface structure. Add to this Trinity Bay's "trained" seagulls, and it is easy to see why Trinity is one of the most heavily-fished bays in the Galveston system.

The other side of the coin is that Trinity Bay, because of its size and distance from the Gulf, is a delicate environment, susceptible to salinity fluctuations that can, quite literally, run the speckled trout out of the area completely. The leading cause of this potential tragedy is the Trinity River. If rainfall to the north is sufficient to swell the Trinity River out of its banks, the salinity of the Bay will be affected. The extent to which it is affected is a contingent upon the duration and magnitude of the flooding. Well, then, you say, let's hope it doesn't rain up there. Wrong, again! Too little rain causes the saline content of the Bay to rise, once again pushing the speckled trout into areas of more desirable salinity. Hope for the right amount of rain, whatever that is. We will discuss how to take advantage of these mishaps of nature later in this section.

As the water temperatures in the spring top 70°, the fish start prowling the shorelines, particularly the southeast shoreline from Smith

Point to Double Bayou. Most believe that the majority of the speckled trout caught in Trinity Bay, the 1^{1}/$_{2}$- to 2-pounders, are transients who have entered the Bay through the Galveston Jetties. These fish will frequent the shorelines until the water temperature passes 83°. From there they go to the deep structure and basically stay there, returning to the shorelines and shallow reefs only during the night.

The wells and reefs closest to the Houston and Trinity Ship Channels produce speckled trout. By late June or early July, Marker 59 on the Houston Ship Channel seems to mark the progress of their northerly migration. From just north of Redfish Island, they continue north past Lost and Tern Reefs (semi-impossible to find in 6 to 9 feet of water) to the Sun Oil Field (and the Getty wells in the same area) southeast of Beazleys Reefs. Then, heading straight up the Bay, they flood through the Amerada Hess Field, into the Exxon-C Lease Field, and on into the Exxon-F Lease Field. After mid- to late-July, the Amerada Hess Field and the Exxon alphabet fields should hold the fish through the remainder of the summer.

Spring is a wader's dream in Trinity, especially the east shoreline. Likely spots to hold fish include Vingt-Et-Un Island, Hodges Reef, Little Hodges Reef (actually a spoil bank, not a reef), the Lone Oak Bayou Area, Double Bayou, Ash Point, and Round Point. The trick is to key in on the presence of bait in the water, or as positive proof, slicks. Boaters drift these same shorelines, anchoring when they find fish. Both groups use artificials, KelleyWigglers, MirrOlures, and 1/2-oz spoons. Boaters and a few waders also use live shrimp under a popping cork. On the western shoreline, most drift from reef to reef—Dow, Beazleys, Fisher Shoals, and Elliots. Waders have frequent success on the North Flats, especially near the HL&P discharge and McCollum Park, as well as Jack's Pocket, which is famous for its redfish on 1/2-oz gold spoons during incoming tides.

Most drift the wells, using shrimp or artificials, to locate the fish. When fish are found, the pros circle back after clearing the area and set up a drift to position the boat where the anchor will be eased overboard. The pads are the target, but the downcurrent edges of the pad are the bulls eyes. It is at these drop-offs where the fish will congregate. Anglers will frequently use shrimp to locate the fish and then switch to KelleyWigglers once the fish are found. This is done for the same reason that shrimptails are used under the birds. It is quicker to release the fish and quicker to get back out there while they are still in the area.

Many bay pros contend the two hours before and after the high stand are the optimum hours for fishing the wells and reefs. Shallow wells, like Exxon F, and shallow reefs, like Beazleys and Fisher Shoals, are frequently best at first light when there is low light and minimum heating of the water. As the day warms, follow the fish to deeper water by moving to deeper shell in the area. The seagulls at Trinity are quite reliable. Some of their more consistent areas of operation include the open bay between Vingt-Et-Un Island and the Sun Oil and Amerada Hess Fields, the area between Cedar and Umbrella Point and these same fields, and the Jack's Pocket area. In the fall, fish hit the shorelines as the water temperature hits 80° and will remain in the area until the water temperature drops into the 60s. Then the pattern reverses, with the fish on the reefs and then the wells.

So what happens when too much rain falls in Trinity Bay? When too much runoff "sweetens" Trinity Bay, the more easily disturbed speckled trout seeks saltier environs. This may ruin the fishing in parts of Trinity Bay, but the fish still have to eat so all it takes is thinking like a speckled trout and knowing where the fish will move. Frequently the Houston Ship Channel is the first spot to try. The flow through the channel forces saltier water from the Gulf to displace and dilute the fresh water from the rivers. If the Trinity and not the San Jacinto River is the culprit, try the Cedar Point Field between Cedar Point and Atkinson Island, as well as the Island's shoreline itself. The Houston Ship Channel, from its juncture with the Trinity River Channel to its intersection with the Bayport Channel, is a prime refuge for the escaping speckled trout. Another ploy is to visually detect the freshwater/saltwater line. If visible, it will be a coloration change most noticeable when a salty incoming tide runs into the fresh water pushed south by the flooding river(s). Speckled trout will stack up on the salty side in a vain attempt to reclaim the territory from which they were evicted. If the flooding is severe enough, the fish may end up in East Bay or even the Jetties. Usually Hannas Reef and/or the Bolivar Wells will offer an acceptable salinity and the required structure to halt the retreat.

Now let's see what happens under drought conditions to the north. Without the "proper" amount of fresh water to dilute the elevated saline levels caused through evaporation and the distance-diminished

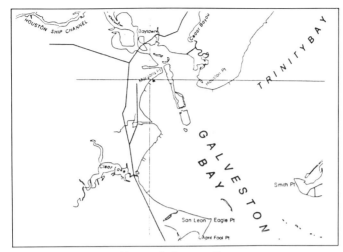

Upper Galveston Bay

Gulf tides, the salinity exceeds the desired levels for the speckled trout. In this scenario, the trout will move into the mouths of the rivers and tributaries. Some of these are Long Island Bayou, Jack's Pass, Blind Bayou, Big and Little Triangle Passes, Southwest Pass, Old River Pass, Kings Pass, Browns Pass, and the Anahuac Channel. As always, the speckled trout are the ones that cannot survive in these conditions. The redfish will still be there, and targeting them instead of their multi-spotted friends can salvage many a fishing trip when Mother Nature's faucet problems have moved the speckled trout back into Galveston County.

Upper Galveston Bay

Location: To us, Upper Galveston Bay is north of April Fool Point (south of Eagle Point at San Leon). We make this statement because we do not have any idea where the "real" boundary is, or if there even is one. It includes the western shoreline and the Houston Ship Channel, the HL&P discharge at Bacliff, numerous reefs and sand flats and continues, again according to us, over to approximately Cedar Point, where Trinity Bay takes over.

Access: Boaters launch from Eagle Point, April Fool Point, Clear Lake, and Baytown's numerous marinas. Waders who go fishing in vehicles that do not float have a variety of places to park and wade. These include the Eagle Point/April Fool Point, Bacliff, San Leon, Kemah, and Seabrook shorelines.

Special Equipment: While access to the water is available, access to shoreline reefs is limited. Bellyboats, those fisherman's innertubes, are widely used to fish the near-shoreline reefs in 5 to 6 feet of water during high tides. Small jonboats are also hand-launched in these areas to achieve the same purpose. Courthouse Reef on the Seabrook Flats is a prime site for these types of boats.

When and Where: San Leon—Take the Gulf Freeway to FM 517, through Dickinson and across Texas 146 into San Leon. Turn right on Broadway and follow it to the water where it becomes Second Street. You can park on this corner or you can go farther south and pull off the road and park. This area is loaded with piers and the remnants of past piers. These provide the structure to which the food chain is connected, small fish eaten by big fish, etc. KelleyWigglers, primarily strawberry cooltail, gold and silver 1/2-oz spoons, MirrOlures, and live shrimp are used here. The pilings, while they attract and hold fish, can also be a real pain in the bait bucket when the wind is blowing. We are sure that we are the only waders who tend to cast onto or over a pier instead of beside it. And it is always in water too deep to wade out and retrieve our errant missile. (We wade here a lot in the spring and fall when waders are required.) Fishing with a popping cork can also provide the wind-driven cork with the opportunity to guide the business end of the rig into a barnacle-encrusted piling instead of the intended prey. For this reason, we usually use fish-finder rigs on the bottom when using live bait. The pilings go almost all the way from Eagle Point to April Fool Point, with some shell scattered along the way. Fish the incoming tide, usually an excellent rule on the flats anywhere on the upper coast.

Seabrook Flats—Take the Gulf Freeway to NASA Road One through Clear Lake and across Texas 146, onto Second Street (same street name, different city) in Seabrook. As you approach Toddville Road on Second, check which way the water is flowing under the small bridge you cross. If it is moving right to left, outflow on the left side, then you have at least one thing going for you. An incoming tide is what you want. At Toddville Road, take a left and go about $1/2$ mile to Hester Street. Turn right onto Hester, avoiding the Honda-sized potholes, and park. The street ends in a bulkhead, over which waders, bellyboaters, and several small jonboats assault the Seabrook Flats and Courthouse Reef, depending upon how tall they are and how well they float. This area does not have the number of pilings that the San Leon shoreline does, but is nonetheless an excellent spot. Wadefishing at night is also popular here. We have caught most of our fish to the right, or south, of Hester Street. Look for bait fish or slicks, moving until you find the fish. All of the Upper Galveston Bay shorelines are protected in a southwest or west wind, providing some of the only fishable water in the area during such conditions.

Bacliff—From Seabrook, take Texas 146 to FM 517, turn left, and in about $1^{1}/2$ miles you will dead-end at the water, east of San Leon. Parking is available there and so is the wading. Concentrate your activity around the pier pilings. Live shrimp and artificials are used here, with shrimp probably being more productive. The fish are usually moving through the area, and shrimp will hold them while artificials will not. You can also take a left on Bayshore Drive and go $1^{1}/2$ miles to the HL&P discharge canal. Heated water (80°) from the generators makes this a winter (as well as fall and spring) hot spot for speckled trout. Most of the fishing here is done with live bait on the bottom, with waders on the adjacent shorelines. There is a lighted pier on one side and a park on the other. Additional information on the pier is found in Chapter 7.

Kemah Flats—Kemah is located on Texas 146, south of Seabrook (across the Clear Lake Bridge). This area is similar to the Bacliff and Seabrook Flats. Fish an incoming tide. The area is protected from southwest winds, and southeast winds frequently drive bait into the area.

Todd's Dump—For most boaters, Todd's Dump is only an obstacle to avoid when launching out of Eagle Point. To the knowledgeable angler, Todd's Dump can be very productive. Todd's Dump is one of the most productive oyster reefs in the Bay for the oystermen, from November to April. Most successful veterans fish the Dump during the weekdays to avoid the crowds of the weekends, with more redfish being caught than speckled trout, probably due to the current cutting through the area. The most productive spot is the unmarked channel running north and south through the reef. This is a current channel and is therefore subject to periodic shifts in location. It is also not that easy to find (which good spots are?). Another productive location is the southeast side of the reef which slopes gently providing the fish a table on which to dine. The other side drops off abruptly into the mud, providing a less desirable dining environ. This tends to make an outgoing tide the more favorable for Todd's Dump.

Houston Ship Channel—The Houston Ship Channel provides spoil-bank fishing that can be excellent. It was, however, not made for fishermen or fish, but ships. These big ships throw off wakes that crash off the spoil banks and have sunk anchored boats with their wakes by swamping the bow of the inattentive boater. Pull anchor and ride out the surge when a ship passes nearby.

Fish are caught in the Channel from the Texas City Dike area all the way to Atkinson Island. Everyone has his favorite markers. Some of ours are 59, 64, and 69. More important than where we have caught fish is how to select a location. The indicators are the same, slicks and mullet; jumping is better than none, but "nervous" water is the best. Nervous bait fish compressed on the surface mean the predators are on the prowl. Jumping mullet means that there are bait fish in the area, and the fish may also be there. Drift the spoilbanks looking for the bait and slip out the anchor when the fish are found.

Live shrimp is probably the most effective bait, under a popping cork, free-shrimped, or on the bottom with a fish-finder rig. Kelley-Wigglers, MirrOlures, and spoons are also used successfully. This type of fishing is basically the shallow-water type. As such, your big motor should not be used to position the boat; drift in and drop the anchor quietly, especially, if other boat traffic is in the area. The Channel is the thoroughfare for tidal movement. Strong tidal movement makes for empty stringers. The days with two highs and two lows (semi-diurnal) tend to be more productive because of the gentler tidal movement, accentuated by the ditch itself.

The Channel is also a haven for fish run out of Trinity Bay because of fluxuations in its salinity. See the section on Trinity Bay for more on this.

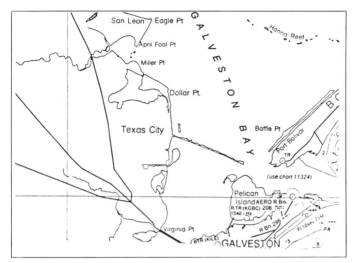

Lower Galveston Bay

Lower Galveston Bay

Location: The upper boundary of Lower Galveston Bay has been proclaimed by us to be April Fool Point. The western boundary is Smith Point, the Bolivar Gas Wells is the southeast boundary, and the Galveston Causeway is the southwest. To the west, it stops at the land.

Access: The Texas City Dike, the Galveston Yacht Basin, and marinas at both ends of the Causeway to Galveston Island. All offer excellent facilities for launching boats and getting bait. Boatless waders can get to the water from the Texas City Dike and Seawolf Park on Pelican Island, across the Galveston Ship Channel from Galveston Island, yielding limited access at best.

Special Equipment: Boat.

When and Where: Dollar Flats—Take the Gulf Freeway to FM 1764. This will take you through Texas City and will dead-end at Bay Street. Take a right and an immediate left and you are on the Texas City Dike. Take a left on the levee. The first couple of miles have been adopted by the wind surfers, but the next three are fair game. This road stops at the flood gates into Moses Lake. Look for green water, bait fish, and/or slicks. Park it and go for it! Best conditions for Dollar Flats include west and southwest winds, southeast winds when bait fish are blown into this pocket, and when Trinity Bay's salinity problems have moved the speckled trout out of the Bay. The best months are generally October through April. As always, live shrimp under a popping cork is popular, with the hardware specialists using KelleyWigglers, $1/2$- and $3/4$-oz spoons in gold and silver, and Mirr-Olures, especially 52MRSHP and 52MR11.

Texas City Dike Flats—Access is from the base of the Texas City Dike. This area centers on the island that is visible north of the jetty near its base. Wade the island to the east and past the far end. Again, look for bait in green water. Wading is successfully done on the north side of the Dike out to about $2/3$ of the way to the end.

Seawolf Park—Take 51st Street from Broadway to the Pelican Island Bridge and Pelican Island. At the end of the Island is Sea Wolf Park, on the site of the old Quarantine Station. Wading is done behind the park on the sand flats and prior to the park along the Galveston Ship Channel. To fish the pier and to have access to the flats behind the Park, you must pay a fee to enter and a fee to fish. We prefer to not pay, and fish the Galveston Channel side prior to the Park. The back flats are better known for flounder than speckled trout. The flats on the channel side have both.

Half Moon Reef—This often-overlooked reef, opposite Dollar Flats, is most productive on moving tides, especially in the summer. We believe the problem is that it is not particularly on the way to anywhere, so most do not know about it, have forgotten about it, or are simply too busy running their big motor to take a side trip for what can be consistent speckled trout fishing.

Moses Lake—Located due south of April Fool Point, north of Texas City, this lake has long been known as a flatfish haven. The secret has been the speckled-trout-and-redfish story. The north, east, and west shorelines can be waded, depending on the winds. There is a deep hole, to 36 feet, on the northeast corner that is a winter hot spot and is productive from October through May for speckled trout, redfish, and flounder. There is a blowout hole just inside the flood gates that hits 40 feet, as well as two channels, one of which complete with spoil banks that hold fish. Marinas are located on its south shoreline and provide food, drinks, and bait. Moses Lake offers protected waters from most winds and is an ideal launch location for the upper part of the Bay. Check it out; we think you will like it.

Other Reefs—Dollar Reef, just off Dollar Point, Levee Reef, off the Texas City Levee between Dollar Point and the Moses Lake floodgates (try the mouth of these gates on an outgoing tide), and Dickinson Reef, between April Fool Point and Miller Point, each can be good, with green water and bait present.

Other Shorelines—Boaters have access to additional productive shorelines. These are the Virginia Point Flats, from the Galveston Causeway at Virginia Point up to and including Campbells Bayou, the opposite shoreline on the north side of Galveston Island from the base of the Causeway for almost 1$^1/2$ miles toward the Pelican Island Bridge, the northeast shoreline of Pelican Island from Seawolf Park almost to the Intracoastal Waterway, and Sand Island, northeast of Pelican Island. The Virginia Point Flats has scattered shell and is known for speckled trout and redfish, except during the hottest summer months. The opposite shoreline is best for speckled trout from October through March. The Pelican Flats produce speckled trout year-round, as do the flats surrounding the peninsula off the west end of Sand Island. Lower Galveston Bay is the easiest to get to, and can put fish in the box for the angler who knows his way around.

West Bay

Location: West Bay runs almost the entire length of Galveston Island, north of the Island from the Causeway to San Luis Pass.

Access: Boaters can launch at several public marinas in the developments on the Bay side of the Island, Pirates Beach, Sea Isle, and Terramar Beach, or they can launch at either of the marinas at the ends of the Causeway. Small boats can launch at a semi-improved ramp on Sportsman's Road off of Anderson Way (8-Mile Road), or the ramp under the bridge over Chocolate Bayou. Boatless waders can gain access to the Bay at the end of Sportsman's Road, next to the private pier at Sea Isle and just east of the San Luis Pass Bridge, plus several other spots in the various developments. Most of these entail a long wade through the mud in the backs of the coves. We believe that the occasional redfish or flounder picked up on those long grueling

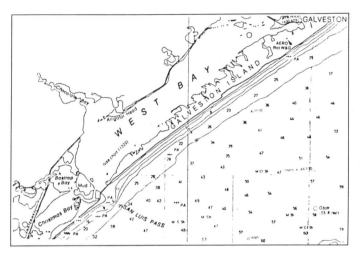

West Bay

wades through the mud are not worth the agonizing effort required to traverse these mud holes.

Services: The above-mentioned marinas all have excellent facilities and usually have bait. To be safe, when launching at a marina in one of the developments, we get bait beforehand from the base of the Causeway to the 71st and 61st Street exits.

When and Where: Because of its importance to the coastal fisherman, we have devoted a separate section to San Luis Pass and the surrounding areas, including the Rooster Collins Flats, Cold Pass, Mud Cut, the Southwest Wall, and the surf at the Pass on Galveston and Follets Island.

To successfully fish West Bay, you need to take into account the seasons, as well as the usual conditions of tide, wind, water temperature, and structure. West Bay fishermen catch two different groups of fish. These are the resident fish who stay in the Bay year-round, and the immigrant fish who enter the Bay from the Gulf in the spring and return to the Gulf during the cold months. This is not to say that these groups do not intermingle, because they do; however, to catch fish throughout the year, you need to know where they are during that particular period.

Winter and early-spring fishermen catch the locals, centered around the eastern half of the Bay, from Carancahua Reef to Confederate Reef and North and South Deer Island. Greens Cut, on the north shoreline, is the center of the action. As the water temperature passes 70° and hits the 76° mark, the invasion of speckled trout from the Gulf to the Bay blows wide open and the fishing focus of the knowledgeable angler shifts from the northeast to the west and eventually to the southwest and San Luis Pass. This is not to say that you cannot catch fish in January at the Pass, or that Anderson Ways does not pay off in the summer, because you can and it does. In the cold months the fish population, especially speckled trout, is significantly smaller in quantity and therefore more localized to a specific area, than it is in the warm months when it is spread out all over the Bay.

At 76°, large speckled trout, the wall-hanger type, enter the surf and the Bay first. This concentration of large fish will remain and peak around the middle of June. After that they begin to leave the Bay, and by the first week in July the trophy fish are gone but more fish are present in the Bay, many in the 2- to 3-lb class—good, solid fish. By mid-July most of the available fish are the 1- to 2-lb models who make up most of our catch through the rest of the summer. Again, these are general guidelines with exceptions pleasantly accepted.

Drift fishing and wading are the two techniques most widely used in West Bay, except when the birds are working, generally from May into June and again from September into November. Some of the more productive drift locations, depending on the wind, are Shell Island to Snake Island, the edges of Carancahua Reef, North and South Deer Islands, from North Deer Island to past Greens Cut, from South Deer Island along Confederate Reef, along the Causeway bridge and railroad bridge, depending upon the current (drift with the tide coming toward you, close to the pilings), and the open bay at the west end behind the Pass, south of Alligator Head and the Old Intracoastal Channel.

Prime wading locations include almost the entire southern shoreline. Look for the salt-grass marshes between the developments, coves, and bayous going into the marshes. Popular wading spots include Terramar Beach to Sea Isle (Little Italy), Sea Isle to Snake Island, Maggies Cove to Shell Island, Shell Island to Carancahua Reef, Carancahua Cove to the Galveston Island State Park, and the Park to the Causeway Bridge. Incoming tides on green water with nervous bait fish are the key for speckled trout. Do not forget the redfish that follow these tides up into the marshes. These can be tough wading because of the mud in the backs of the coves, but tailing redfish in the marshes on gold weedless spoons go a long way toward making you forget those aching leg muscles. As the tide turns, the mouths of the canals and bayous coming out of the marshes are the places to get another crack at the ones you missed the first time.

The boatless waders have a long walk to a lot of these spots; however, they can still wade some of them and still catch fish in West Bay. Following are several of the spots available to park and wade.

Anderson Ways—Anderson Ways, or 8-Mile Road, can be reached from Stewart Road, the second traffic light on 61st from Broadway, or from San Luis Road, which goes from Seawall Boulevard to San Luis Pass. Turn right and follow it almost to the end. Turn left on Sportsman's Road, take it to the end, and park. The shoreline continues to your left to an inlet. This inlet and around the back of the island is fished mostly by flounder fishermen. The inlet can be waded when you are not wearing waders. The deepest part is very narrow. We frequently wade this gut and then walk along the island, the first half which is salt grass, to get to the area where there are a series of sand and shell beaches. This area has several shell reefs and a hard sand bottom.

In warm weather we take this route because the area immediately in front of where you park and basically down almost to the beaches on the small island is mud and sand and not very productive; however, the real reason to do so is to avoid the stingrays! Big ones, little ones, if you like stingrays, you are going to love this place! The first time we fished this area with our mad-banker friend, Don Robinson, we had stayed out a little too long trying to duplicate the stringer of speckled trout and redfish which another wader had, quite smugly, shown us. We were shuffling our way back in, in the dark, having caught one redfish, no speckled trout, and 6 or 8 stingrays (thus the shuffling). As we approached the safety of the bank, we were startled (to say the least) by a loud bang, which immediately drew our attention to a circular mud boil, about 3 feet in diameter, 6 feet in front of us. The banker thought we had tripped and fallen into the water, it was that loud! We knew immediately what had happened. We were able to tell him what it was later, after our hearts got out of our throats and we were again able to speak. We had kicked the tail of a huge stingray (the kind that, instead of wrapping its tail around your leg and pushing its barb into your ankle, will wrap its tail around your waist and stick its barb in more sensitive areas!) that was sitting in about 18 inches of water, three feet from the bank! Since then, we have also broken one 7-foot graphite rod (LCI 704) exactly in half, trying to beach another rather large stingray (2 feet in diameter). Now we will answer your two questions. The first answer is no; we are not absolutely insane. The second answer is yes; we do catch a lot of speckled trout and redfish in this area. If you want to catch fish, you go where the fish are!

When wearing waders, you can walk in front of the channel without any depth change. The first reef is before the first beach. Another reef, or piece of the same reef, runs into the Bay from the point of the first beach. From there on, there is scattered shell along the remainder of the small island. Fish the whole area for speckled trout, and concentrate on the reefs and scattered shell for redfish.

This area gets its tidal movement from the Galveston Jetties, not San Luis Pass. With an incoming tide and south or southeast winds, it is best to use a popping cork to cover the whole area, walking as your cork drifts right to left, with the wind allowing long casts. We, because we are clever, call this drift wading. It is a different story on the way back. The tide takes about 30 minutes from the time it starts moving at the Jetties to reach this area. The best fishing is on an incoming tide. For those of you who do not care to wade in wall-to-wall stingrays, there is hope. Maybe the sharks will eventually eat all of them. Yes, there are also sharks there in the summer, but they are the small, ankle-biter, black-tip variety that are fun to catch, good to eat, and a good way to have a little fun if the more respectable species are not cooperating. Just catch a pinfish, cut off its dorsal fin, put on a wire leader and a single hook, and throw it out there under a cork. You may even get lucky and catch a big speckled trout or redfish on this rig.

Sea Isle—Take San Luis Road to the entrance of Sea Isle, turn right and take the road, following a jog to the right and left, to the resident's private fishing pier. Park there and wade in at the base of the pier. We have not had much success in the cove beside the pier. We either wade across the cove and work the shoreline, or wade out along the pier and fish the waist-deep flats.

The next major cove is Snake Island Cove. There is a major bayou that feeds the back of Snake Island Cove just west of the Cove. It has a small island at its mouth. It has some shell scattered around it, and frequently holds redfish. The bayou mouth, between the small island and Galveston Island, holds speckled trout and redfish as the tide starts to come out of the marsh. These are frequently small, but usually good for a few keepers on the fall of a spring tide. In Snake Island Cove, look for bait fish and/or slicks. Work the open end for speckled trout, and the back of the Cove, in the mud, and the canals and ditches going back onto the marsh for redfish. This marsh is one of the few places we have stalked tailing redfish in the Galveston Bay system. There is nothing in bay fishing that compares to the exhilaration of creeping into position in the mud to put a weedless gold spoon ahead of the nose of a redfish, a portion of whose tail is sticking 6 inches out of the water. You are not always successful, but when you are through, you are, at least, left with a uniquely exciting memory.

Offatts Bayou—Owing to this area's unique features, it will be covered in the section on Cold Weather Fishing found in Chapter 7.

Halls Lake, Greens Lake, and Jones Lake—These are all too shallow to support fish in the summer. Jones and Greens Lakes are, however, known for excellent fishing under the birds in the spring, even though they are primarily considered redfish territory on spring tides in the spring and fall.

Pines Plaza Sporting Goods' Pertinent Fact:

* 34 percent of all monthly winners were caught in West Bay. East Bay was second with 25 percent.

Satellite Bays: Chocolate, Bastrop, and Christmas Bays—Chocolate Bay is shallow with a mud and shell bottom. It is primarily redfish territory, but if you can find some deep water, you may find speckled trout. This bay is shallow and should be navigated slowly unless you are with a local expert. Shallow-draft scooters are the primary means of transportation for the serious Chocolate Bay redfisherman.

Drifting is the primary technique for the boaters. Bastrop and Christmas Bays are separated from West Bay by large salt-grass marsh islands, the largest of which are Mud Island and Moodys Island. Water access to these Bays is through Guyton (Mud) Cut, Cold Pass, and Titlum Tatlum Bayou, with Cold Pass the deepest.

These Bays are also known for redfish, but speckled trout ride the spring tides in during the spring and fall. Bastrop Bay is drifted or worked by wading the spoil banks and shorelines where you can find sand and/or shell instead of the usual mud.

Christmas Bay is the easiest to reach by boat, through Cold Pass, or worked by car from FM 3005, the Blue Water Highway. Go approximately $3^{1}/_{2}$ miles from the Freeport side of the San Luis Pass bridge and turn north toward the Bay on a barely distinguishable path directly adjacent to a clump of small cedar bushes. This trail can have puddles that are possibly bigger than your car, but the bottom is hard sand. If you have a reasonable ground clearance (we drive trucks) then you should not have a problem. There is another access point $6^{1}/_{2}$ miles from the bridge.

Christmas Bay has two different types of fish habitats. The shoreline is mud and sand with some scattered shell. Frequently there is also floating grass in the water. This is redfish territory, and is fished most easily with $1/_{2}$-oz weedless gold spoons. About 100 yards from the shoreline, there is a small drop-off and you will be on hard sand and in speckled trout territory. The speckled trout are usually small, except during the spring and fall when big speckled trout chase the mullet through Cold Pass and into Christmas Bay. Because of the shallow water in these Bays, be especially conscious of when the high tides are scheduled to fall and make sure you are on the way out also. He who gets caught by a norther in there may have to wait for spring (season, not tide).

San Luis Pass

Location: San Luis Pass, the largest natural pass on the Texas Coast, located between the west end of Galveston Island and Follets Island.

Access: FM 3005, San Luis Pass Road on Galveston Island, and the Blue Water Highway on Follets Island each end at the toll bridge over San Luis Pass. Boaters may launch at the old KOA campgrounds or at a public ramp 3 miles from the bridge on Follets Island, or at any of the marinas on Galveston Island. Boatless waders have access from both sides of the bridge and from a parking lot on West Bay beside the

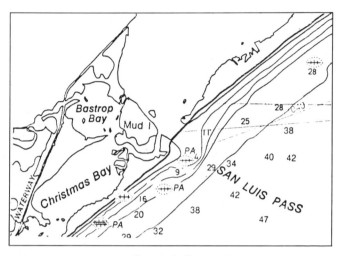

San Luis Pass

westernmost sewage-treatment plant, about 1/2 mile from the bridge on the Galveston Island side.

Services: Minimal. Bait should be obtained in Surfside or Galveston prior to heading for the Pass.

Special Equipment: Life preserver.

When and Where: When the crusty old salt cleaning a limit of speckled trout tells you that he caught them at "the Pass," bear in mind that he could have been in the surf a mile either side of the Pass, in West Bay anywhere from Bay Harbor to the Pass, or anywhere from the Pass itself up to the Intracoastal Waterway at Chocolate Bay. That is the immediate area directly and instantaneously impacted by what happens at San Luis Pass. When we were kids, we heard our fathers discuss San Luis Pass with something like reverence in their voices. We knew that was where the big fish were and where the big boys fished. We knew that "the Pass" was where we were going to fish when we grew up. Well, we still have not grown up, but we definitely have and will continue to fish the Pass. Fishing the Pass means fishing three different areas: the surf, the Pass itself, and West Bay near the Pass.

The surf means wading, and surf wading is to fishing what goose hunting is to the waterfowler. It means getting chest- to neck-deep in water with waves breaking over your head, tossing brightly-colored lures into a green gut full of skittish mullet. It means getting after the fish in an environment to which they are infinitely better suited. But, to the avid fisherman, the difficulties pale in comparison to the rewards.

Some of the more productive areas for fishing the surf are as follows:

- The third bar on either side of the Pass.
- The Freeport Bar. Keep in mind that it is extremely dangerous and should be attempted only by an expert swimmer wearing a life vest with another angler similarly qualified and equipped.
- The Cars, an artificial reef originally placed there to prevent beach erosion. In that it now attracts speckled trout to the Follets Island surf, we can assume that the idea did not work as well as was planned. It is located 1½ miles from the Pass.
- The Boilers, a wreck located 4 miles west of the Pass. It is best for speckled trout in the spring and summer, and redfish in the fall.
- The Cedars, an area of shell marked by a large group of cedar trees on the shore, 5 miles west of the Pass.
- The Shrimpers, a series of 3 wrecked shrimp boats farther down the Follets Island surf that each produce fish. Fish the guts between the wrecks for speckled trout and an occasional redfish.

On the Galveston Island side of the Pass, the suds-busting is best at the following locations:

- The Pilings, located from the Pass to just west of the Bay Harbor subdivision, where a series of pilings goes from the surf up to the beach.
- Sea Isle development, near the center of a 3-mile stretch of sand and shell, is also productive.

The surf is dependent upon the wind to be productive. Southeast winds under 10 knots will provide the green incoming tides and the 18 inches of water visibility required to hit the surf looking for bait and that one big fish (or a bunch of not-so-big fish).

Fishing the Pass itself can be done by boat or by wading. Wading should be done only on the Galveston Island side, where the drop-off is gradual. The Freeport side has an immediate drop-off from which fishermen take their last step on earth each year. That is correct; one too many steps toward the Pass, or not enough steps backward quickly enough, and they drown, life preserver or not. *Do not wade at the Pass on the Freeport side!* Anglers cast toward the pier pilings on the downcurrent side to catch the fish hiding out of the current behind the pilings. Another technique is to cast a popping cork into the current ahead of the piling, and then play the line so the bait is taken behind the piling by the current.

Now we move into West Bay behind the Pass, in a boat. Inside the Pass, east of Bird Island, is a large area of sand flats that changes with every tide. These bars can be waded, but *you must leave a person in the boat* to rescue any wader who discovers that the 3-foot gut he crossed to get to the rapidly-dissolving bar on which he is standing is now a 20-foot deep raging torrent between him and the boat. Needless to say, the person in the boat should know how to operate it well and quickly. This series of guts is where the speckled trout play hide-and-seek with the schools of mullet. The mouth of Titlum Tatlum Bayou and on out into Cold Pass' mouth are excellent locations, especially on an outgoing tide. Bird Island on its north shoreline is excellent on incoming tides in the spring. Mud Cut is another outgoing tide ambush point. It is also the southern boundary of the area called the Southwest Wall. This area should be drifted because of a mud bottom. Redfish are caught here, but this is one of the more recognized big speckled trout areas. The spoil islands, from Alligator Head east along the Intracoastal Waterway, are summertime hangouts for speckled trout.

The wader without a boat can turn off San Luis Road to the right about 1/2 mile before the bridge, and park in a parking lot next to the westernmost sewage treatment plant. The wader has several options upon entering the water. About 200 yards offshore there is a gut. This gut is about a 1/2 mile long, ending in mud to the left of the parking lot toward the Pass and flattening out again at a point just before the easternmost of the two treatment plants. This gut can be fished on any moving tide. We prefer to fish it as the tide turns and starts to gain momentum. This gut can be good for a couple of hours.

On big incoming tides we wade parallel to the gut, fishing it as we move to the east. If we see a lot of bait on the flats ahead of us, we continue in that direction. If not, we head toward the open Bay.

Approximately $1/4$ mile out there is a large bar marked by stakes. We wade the eastern edge of it until we hit the gradual drop-off to deeper water. We then wade into waist-deep water and turn back to parallel the drop-off. A stake marks the northern corner of this area, and we wade toward it. We have had excellent success with speckled trout and redfish on this wade to the stake. You can then either turn around and do it again or continue around the corner to the left. On the east and south sides of the flats are a series of guts that can be worked as well as the flats themselves. You can proceed around the south side of the flat and return where you came in at the easternmost plant. It is a long stroll, but it can be quite a productive walk.

Many lures are used with success at San Luis Pass. Our favorites are strawberry cooltail KelleyWigglers, $1/2$- and $3/4$-oz spoons in gold and silver, MirrOlures, of which the 28, 752, 704, 11, and 12 are our favorites, and broken-back Cotton Cordell Redfins in silver/black back and silver/blue back. In strong currents we go to $1^1/4$-oz Tony Acceta spoons, KelleyWigglers, and 60- and 65- series MirrOlures. Live shrimp, especially big shrimp, are also killers. We also use finger mullet, small croakers, and pinfish when we are intent on that one big fish, which is always a possibility when fishing San Luis Pass.

MATAGORDA BAY AREA

Matagorda Bay is actually two bays: East and West. Both East Matagorda and West Matagorda Bays are interesting areas for us to summarize because they represent such a wide diversity of habitat for speckled trout and redfish. It is on this section of the Texas coast that the Colorado River flows from the town of Matagorda into the Gulf of Mexico, thereby effectively splitting what was once believed to be one bay into the two bays we have today. Because they are separate, they have different characteristics and are, in a number of ways, fished differently.

East Matagorda Bay

Directions: There are two ways to approach East Matagorda Bay. From Bay City, drive southeast on Highway 457 past Sargent to the

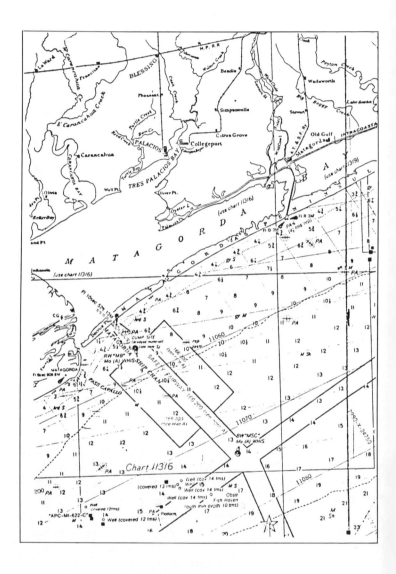

MATAGORDA BAY AREA

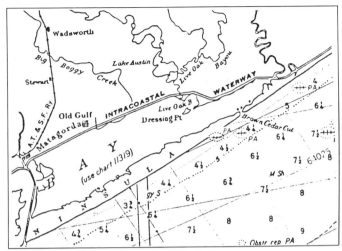

East Matagorda Bay

Intracoastal Waterway. This will put you near the east end of East Bay. To reach the west end of the bay, drive south on Highway 60 from Bay City to the town of Matagorda.

Access: For wadefisherman, drive south from Matagorda on FM 2031 (beach road) to the mouth of the Colorado River and turn left onto the beach. We recommend this to 4-wheel-drive-equipped wadefishermen only. From there it is about 20 miles of beach to the Caney Creek Channel to the Gulf, and of that about 15 miles of hard sand and shell bottom to wade in the Bay. As you drive down the beach, look to your left for cuts to wells to gain access to the Bay itself.

By boat, we recommend putting in at C&R Marina on the Intracoastal Waterway at Matagorda. From there you travel down the Intracoastal heading east, to a series of cuts that provide access to the Bay. The first of these is Old Gulf Cut (about 5 miles) followed by Boggy Bayou (about 9 miles) and then a series of cuts referred to as the Flounder Cut (about 11–12 miles). Remember these distances are from Matagorda, so you might consider launching at Holiday Beach Marina on the Intracoastal below Sargent to reduce your boat ride if you intend to fish the areas east of the Flounder Cut.

Services: Both of the marinas provide fairly complete services, but we recommend not waiting to "stock up" until you have only one supplier and are 100 miles from home.

Special Equipment: For those of you who are naturally adverse to critters-of-the-deep bites, close encounters of the stingray kind, or simply do not want to loose the crease in your fishing pants, a boat is required. You should keep in mind, however, that most of East Matagorda Bay is less than 4-feet deep and is therefore excellent wadefishing territory. The hardware of choice is shallow-running topwater lures (51MR series MirrOlures or broken-back redfins) and an assortment of shrimptail jigs. (See Chapter 2 for specific colors and sizes.) We recommend fishing shrimptail jigs under a Mansfield Mauler attached about 18 inches above the jig.

When and Where: Because East Matagorda Bay is so shallow, water temperature and wind become critical factors to consider. Our favorite conditions (which most often occur yesterday, when we were somewhere else) are a light south-southeast wind, spring temperatures gradually warming the flats to 75°, and moving water from either an incoming or outgoing tide.

For drift fishing, we recommend starting at St. Marys Bayou. This area can tolerate a southwest or west wind and will produce both redfish and speckled trout. Next, we suggest drifting the reefs. Begin with an area known as Raymond Landing. As always, look for bait fish or bird activity (or both) and fish the downcurrent side first. Other names to look for on your fishing map in this area are Raymond Reef, Long Reef, and Beacon Reef. Next, try Deep Reef. This area often provides clearer water because it is somewhat closer to the protected shoreline (provided there is a south or southeast wind). Further east, and in the approximate center of East Bay, is Drew's Hump (seen on some maps as Drull's Lump). As the water in East Bay begins to warm up, Drew's Hump is one of the areas where fish may concentrate to escape the heat. Continuing east (and this is an area you might want to approach from the Caney Creek direction), try the Oil Well Pads (known to some as the Oyster Farm Reefs). Drift around each of the reefs and remember, if the desire hits you, this is an excellent area to wade. Halfmoon Shoal is known by the locals as Plow Shear Reef. It seems once upon a time someone (maybe a local farmer) marked this reef with a series of plow shears. Later, we understand, someone painted them red so there was no question that these were the right plow shears sticking up in East Matagorda Bay. Time has taken its toll on the plow shears, but the reef remains a consistent producer of fish. Bird Island and Bird Island Reefs, as well as Chinquapin Reefs, can be good too, but like the North Shore Reef and the north shoreline back to Boggy Bayou, they are best at high tide.

For wadefishermen this is a great area. From St. Marys down to 3-Mile Reef, you will find speckled trout and redfish over the grassy shell-and-mud bottom. Be sure and work the sloughs, creeks, and bayous on the shore. On the south shore of East Bay from 3-Mile Reef, all the way to the Brown Cedar Cut area, you will find what we consider to be prime wading country. Our favorite spots are Boiler Bayou, Hog Island, and Eidelbach Flats. When you find a gut or significant change in water depth or bottom, work that area hard. Also be sure and fish the inlets. Generally you will find the inlet bottoms to be very soft but when redfish are working them, they can provide great action.

West Matagorda Bay

West Matagorda Bay is significantly larger than is East Matagorda Bay. We will only summarize that part of the bay from the town of Matagorda to Palacios Point on the north, and on the south shore to a concrete bulkhead 4 miles past Greens Bayou.

As we wrote this edition of Pocket Guide, we watched a channel being dug by the U.S. Army Corp of Engineers. This project was designed to redirect the flow of the Colorado River into the eastern end of West Matagorda Bay. The reason(s) for digging the channel, at least to us, were not really clear. Even though we are not experts in hydrology, it seems to us that substantial freshwater influx into a somewhat delicate saltwater estuary would have a noticeable effect. Without a "new and improved" opening to the Gulf, this area could very likely change in the next few years. But we will summarize it "as is."

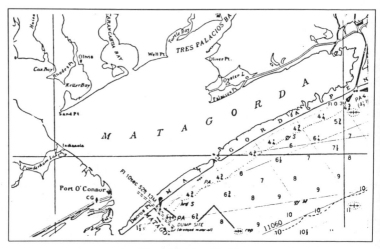

West Matagorda Bay

Directions: West Matagorda Bay (the part we will summarize) is reached by going first to the town of Matagorda, Texas (20 miles south of Bay City, Texas on Highway 60).

Access: You may launch at C & R Marina on the Intracoastal Waterway in Matagorda, or at Rawling's Bait Camp, Allen's Landing, or the Riverbend Tavern and Bait Camp, all of which are on the Colorado River. Riverbend is the only public boat ramp. After launching, head west down the Intracoastal Waterway if you launched at C&R Marina, or down the Colorado River if you launched at Rawling's, Allen's, or Riverbend Marinas. Access to the Bay from the Colorado is through Parkers Cut, but only at high tide. Another approach is down the Intracoastal about 3 miles to Culver Cut. Both of these routes provide access to the extreme east end of the Bay.

When and Where: For the drift fisherman, we suggest working a reef just to the left of the channel coming out of Culver Cut. This used to be a very productive area prior to the dredging and can still produce fish. To find it, we recommend looking for the channel itself or any obvious signs of bait in the area. Incoming and high tides are best, and a southeast wind is our best choice. Next, head for Shell Island Reef on the north shore and fish back to Culver Cut. Set up your drift so that you can throw in between the islands. Twin Islands and the reefs that run between them are great places for speckled trout to ambush their prey, particularly at the drop-off on the east side. This cut is also a steady live-bait area.

Another point at which you can enter West Matagorda Bay from the Intracoastal is through Mad Island Cut about 10 miles west of Matagorda. Mad Island Reef is west of the channel through the cut. Both sides can be productive particularly when water is moving through the cut (either outgoing or incoming tide, but not slack). The next stop on the north shore heading west is Round Reef. Here you will find a mud-and-shell bottom around the reef itself. We recommend fishing it with shrimptail jigs or Johnson Sprites ($1/2$- or $1/4$-oz). The further you get from Round Reef, the more grass you will find. Try a Mansfield Mauler about 18 inches above your shrimptail jig. The last recommended area to drift is Halfmoon Reef. It runs in a southwesterly direction from Palacios Point for about 3 miles. This area can be very productive after the flats are too warm to hold fish.

For the wader, we strongly recommend the south shore of West Matagorda Bay. Begin at the tide gauge in front of Golds Bayou and work anywhere on the south shore heading southwest all the way to a concrete bulkhead. This structure is hard to miss, but for reference it is about 4 miles south of Greens Bayou. The length of this area is fished the same, with few exceptions, from start to finish. Almost the entire area has the same bottom conditions: hard sand, shell, and some mud in the backs of the many bayous.

One closing note about West Matagorda Bay—A local guide once said he thought he understood why his bay was not as heavily fished as other areas along the Texas Coast. He suggested that most fishermen who have tried it as an alternative to Galveston Bay rarely spend the time it takes to really learn it. We wholeheartedly agree! Any area worth fishing is worth studying until you really know it. If you are only going to be there once, call a guide and use his knowledge. We believe the guides listed in the Appendix will help, but there is just no substitute for time on the water.

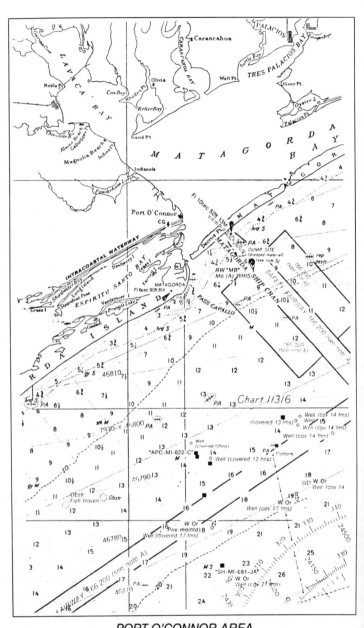

PORT O'CONNOR AREA

PORT O'CONNOR AREA

Directions: Port O'Connor is very easy to find because it's on the way to nowhere except the end of Highway 185 and, more importantly, great fishing. From Port Lavaca head south on Highway 238 and then left on FM 1289 until it dead-ends into Highway 185. Turn left and go about 5 miles until the pavement turns to water. Then stop.

Access: To fish Port O'Connor effectively you must have a boat. Launching facilities on the Intracoastal Waterway include Doc's Dock, Bobbie's Bait Camp, and P.O.C. Bait and Tackle, all of which are full-service marinas. From these marinas you can go east and fish the back side of the Matagorda Peninsula, or go in a southeasterly direction and fish the Port O'Connor back bays.

Special Equipment: Boat.

When and Where: Port O'Connor is the point on the Texas coast where we begin to see activity in pursuit of speckled trout and redfish almost all year long. We've heard many stories about casting to tailing redfish from a duck blind in the month of December. We believe one reason for this is Port O'Connor's close proximity to 30- to 40-foot depths of the open Gulf and sizeable Pass Cavallo, which allows continuous restocking of the back bays. Our summary of this rich year-round area will cover from the concrete bulkhead on the back side of Matagorda Peninsula just west of Greens Bayou and continue in a southwesterly direction to Cedar Bayou.

From Greens Bayou through an area known as Airport Flats and onto the Jetties, we fish a hard sand bottom with scattered shell. All through this area guts that divide sand bars or reefs run parallel to the shore. This area is generally best in the spring and fall, particularly with a southeast wind. Add to that an outgoing tide and all those little lakes you see on a fishing map will begin to release their supply of menhaden, shrimp, crabs, and other bait fish, much to the delight of waiting speckled trout and redfish. From the Jetties to Decros Point you will also find a hard sand bottom, but this area is best when fished in April and May. Best baits for this area are shrimptail jigs, Blakemore worms (Double Trouble), Swimming Shad fished under a Mansfield Mauler, and weedless spoons. This area is really best when waded, but can be fished from a boat. Set up your drift to cover the area from the grass line to the drop-off to deeper water. Continuing around Decros Point, go about 1 mile east on the south shore of the peninsula. From this point almost back to the Jetties is some of the most productive surf fishing in the area, for that matter, on the entire Texas Coast. Best baits for the surf are 52MR26 and 52MR28 MirrOlures and big 1¹/₄-oz gold spoons. This area can yield some of the largest speckled trout and redfish Port O'Connor will see all year, but is best during the spring and fall.

Before we cross Pass Cavallo, we would like to raise a caution flag for wadefishermen. On a calm day a guy can wade chest deep-water most of the morning and not have any problem at all. But after taking a sandwich break for 20 to 30 minutes on the beach, he can return to the water only to find out there is now an outgoing tide with which to deal. If you recall the recommendation in the equipment section of this Pocket Guide, you will remember something about having a life preserver. Pass Cavallo is probably the best reason we can give you for having and using one. The Pass and the Port O'Connor Jetties should be fished from a boat.

Once past Pass Cavallo, you will find 34 miles of the most beautiful of Texas beaches. Because access is limited to Matagorda Island, this area tends to accumulate an amazing assortment of shells. (See, we really do look at things other than our corks.) When fishing this stretch of surf, look for structure such as wadeable sand bars (fish the guts in between), shell reefs, and especially sunken wrecks. Of course, working birds, exploding bait fish, and nervous water are always our preferred signs.

Returning to the point at which we started our summary, let's now review the back bays. Fishermans Cut is the opening at the east end of Blackberry Island through which you enter Barroom Bay from the Intracoastal at Port O'Connor. The area from Fishermans Cut to Little Marys Cut has a soft mud bottom but is good for reds in the early spring and fall. Use live bait, such as shrimp under a popping cork. Continue heading southwest to an area called Mitchells Cut. There is a fairly well-maintained channel here and you can find good black-drum fishing in the early spring. We prefer to use crab on a single hook, fished on the bottom. On the south side of Blackberry Island, from Everett Reef all the way to Military Cut.

you will find a hard sand bottom good for speckled trout and redfish (and flounder in the fall). Look for Bill Days Reef on your map. Its north side is soft mud and the south side is hard sand. This "full service" reef seems to have something for everyone and should definitely be one of your targets for the day. Continuing west along the south shores of Dewberry and Long Islands, you will find a hard sand bottom and excellent wading. Pay particular attention to the small cuts from the lagoon and Shoalwater Bay into Espiritu Santo Bay. These cuts are the place to be when a high tide turns to go out. At the far west end of Espiritu Santo Bay you should wade a series of reefs that run from Little Grass Island, around Steamboat Island, and on south to the First Chain of Islands. This entire area will provide good wading as fish move in and out of deeper water in the bays via the flats around each island and through South Pass.

To cover the east end and the south shore of Espiritu Santo, begin where Mitchells Cut meets Saluria Bayou near the Old Coast Guard Station ruins. This area is due south of Barroom Bay. As you travel west on Saluria, Bayucas Island is on your right. Follow its south shore around to Teller Point. The area between Teller Point, Bayucas Point, and Grass Island is great for redfish year-round. The bottom is soft mud and grass. This can be tough fishing. For a breather, go south to Farwell Island and drift the north and south sides (or leeward side).

When you drift this or any other area at Port O'Connor, be aware of two things. (1) There are generally three different bottom conditions in the back bays: hard sand (sometimes with grass), oyster-shell reefs, and mud. Each condition is affected differently by water movement, light, and wind. A bottom covered with grass may remain clear under strong winds, but as soon as the grass has had an opportunity to absorb some of the sun's light, it begins to rise off the bottom and can render that area considerably less fishable. One solution to this of course, is the Mansfield Mauler, which tends to keep a shrimptail jig from becoming fouled in the grass. A mud bottom is usually the last to clear, but that can mean prime redfish habitat. Since reds feed by smell, clarity is not generally an issue. An oyster-shell reef tends to act as a buffer for off-color water moving through a bay, but only for a limited length of time. This is why during particularly windy weather, the leeward or downwind side of a reef will often provide water clear enough for speckled trout to set up their ambush. (2) When drifting, the intensity with which you cover an area is less than when you wade. The advantage to drifting is you cover more area in a specified time and, as a result, increase your chances of locating fish. Once they have been located you have several options—repeat the drift, anchor, or get out and wade. Can you tell that we are somewhat biased toward wadefishing? For us, covering an area thoroughly is of utmost importance, and we have yet to think of a worthwhile reason to hurry when we are fishing.

From here we suggest you try Big Pocket, a cove due east of Farwell Island. Great wadefishing territory for tailing reds. And with prevailing south/southeast winds, you will usually find fishable water. From Big Pocket, heading approximately west, you can fish the south shoreline of Espiritu Santo, which provides some 9 miles of mostly hard sand bottom. As you make this trek, there are several hot spots to try. The first of these is Army Hole. Probably best known for its prowess as a top winter-fishing spot, Army Hole has provided incredible results at the most unlikely times. Once past a somewhat shallow entrance you will find a significantly deeper protected lake. With ice on everything above the water line, brave winter souls have in past years and pre-GCCA inspired restrictions, significantly bruised the speckled trout and redfish population. A guide once told us (with glazed eyes, sweaty palms, and a neck twitch we had never seen before), "It was like tuna fishin' in the North Atlantic."

The next few miles are like the last two—great! This shore is actually on Vandeveer Island, south of which is Pringle Lake. On an outgoing tide the three cuts through Vandeveer Island provide points of escape to the Bay. Fish the outside (Bay side) of these cuts on a falling tide. Generally, any mullet imitation, shrimptail jig, or spoon will get their attention. Keep in mind that when fishing this clear water the dark water/dark lure, light water/light lure rule applies. We do not believe in any hard-and-fast rules regarding lure selection when it comes to color. There are good performers year in and year out so you should try them. If you want someone's advice, ask one of the guides listed in the Appendix. They were out there yesterday and can probably narrow your selection in a hurry.

Pringle Lake is the reason the skinny water boats were invented. If you do not believe it, just show up at Pringle on a morning when the wind is less than 10 mph in April and witness the swarming of the Scooters. The lake itself is wadeable—so are the Florida Everglades—but drifting is by far our first choice. Pringle Lake can and regularly does hold enormous numbers of speckled trout and redfish. Because most of the lake is very shallow and relatively protected from the wind, fish are easy to spot. As a result, you can cast to specific fish as you spot them. When a 28-inch redfish hits your gold spoon in 10 inches of water, you are in for an experience that Port O'Connor regulars have enjoyed for years. And it does not stop at Pringle. Contee Lake, South Pass Lake, Long Lake, Corey Cove, and Pats Bay offer similar conditions. The three lakes are considerably smaller, but each has its own character. For the bulletproof wader, there is a marsh inland of these three lakes. The loner can find ample privacy in search of tailing reds.

It is at about this point that you leave Espiritu Santo Bay and enter San Antonio Bay. Even though the name changes, the conditions are practically the same. You will find more wadeable shell reefs and should fish this area the same way. On your map find Panther Point. This area is where Chandeleur Island's guide Rudy Grigar, out of Louisiana, made a name for himself. It's about 22 miles from Port O'Connor, and this distance helps minimize the number of anglers. We suspect fish found here enter Mesquite Bay (the next one to the south) through Cedar Bayou. A lot of people who fish between Cedar Bayou and Panther Point will tell you this is where the monster fish live. Specifically, Panther Point Lake and Swan Lake (in the back) may very well prove this local rumor to be true.

Cedar Bayou regulars, on the other hand, make no such claims. It does provide access from the Gulf to Mesquite Bay, but only for fish. After a long ride you will only be able to get within about 500 yards of the Gulf-side mouth of Cedar Bayou. We can tell you the surf outside this pass can be the most aggressive area to fish we have found. On our last visit to this surf one of us tied into what must have been a world-class jack crevalle and within about $1/2$ a second lost everything except the garment that has the fruit label in the back. Somehow, when you're dressed like this, it's very disconcerting to know there's a wild MirrOlure thrashing madly in the surf.

We have not mentioned two other areas in the vicinity of Port O'Connor: Port Lavaca and Seadrift. Under ideal conditions, the bays adjacent to each of these communities can and often do produce fish. We have also noticed, however, that most of the locals from these towns (even the few guides that live there) chose to fish either Matagorda Bay, the back bays at Port O'Connor, or Espiritu Santo Bay. After fishing both areas, we completely agree that if given the opportunity to fish the waters adjacent to Port O'Connor, we would do just that. In our judgment, Port O'Connor offers more protected water with structure and more wadeable areas as well.

Now if all the areas talked about in this summary do not produce fish, there is one more place to try. The Port O'Connor Jetties offer several differences in terms of structure, depth, and water movement. They are located about 3 miles across Matagorda Bay from Port O'Connor. Originally, these jetties were built to reinforce a cut made through the Matagorda Peninsula between the Bay and the Gulf. The water depth is about 60 to 65 feet on the Gulf end of the Jetties, and the average depth at the base of the rocks is in the neighborhood of 30 feet. This means a tremendous amount of water moves from the Gulf to Matagorda Bay and back again in the course of a day. With this movement of water comes a continuing supply of food upon which speckled trout and redfish feed.

Most Port O'Connor guides and knowledgeable jetty fishermen recognize all this natural food as formidable competition and use live bait. This can be shrimp, croaker, or mullet. Shrimp is usually fished under a popping cork rigged at about 8 or more feet, or allowed to drift "free" with the current. One of our favorite rigs for the Jetties is to use live croaker as the bait. We cut the dorsal fin from the croaker's back, and using a 2/0 or 3/0 hook just in front of our incision, allow the fish to swim freely. Live mullet are fished the same way but no surgery is performed here. The single hook is used, but this time it's put through the lips.

In deeper water you may find some surprises. There are big fish here; both bull redfish and trophy speckled trout (as well as other species). For this reason we recommend at least 14-lb test line and a shock leader section of at least 20-lb test line.

Any time there is water movement, especially in the spring and fall, a drift parallel to the rocks can produce good numbers of speckled trout and redfish. Because of the depth of water, other fish move from the shallows on the flats to the Jetties to escape the heat in midsummer. Large schools of fish can concentrate here and the action can be fast and furious when they are found. It is at this point during a trip to the Jetties that you may consider anchoring. It sure provides a good break in the action and remember, you never know what might swim by at the Jetties of Port O'Connor.

Well, that just about covers Port O'Connor, but we want to make a couple of small points. The first is about the special people of this special town. For accommodations we recommend Gayle Wilson's Tarpon Motel. He understands fishermen and can be reached at (512) 983-2606. For condo or house rentals call our friend Ron (or his better-half, Mary Ann) Claiborne with Coastal Real Estate at (512) 983-2296. If you are bitten by the permanent bug and must become a property owner, Ron can help with that too. What a guy!

The second point we would like to make has to do with bait and lures. All through this summary we have recommended artificials. On the flats at Port O'Connor we have found all artificials will, at some time, do the job. As a matter of fact, they are still our first choice. However, when fishing is slow and fish are hard to find, our guides use live bait. This seems to be more effective on the rocks at the Jetties (free shrimping) and under a popping cork over reefs. When the water is off color, live bait can provide a definite advantage, especially for redfish.

CHAPTER 5

ORGANIZATIONS

Several months ago we were amused by a conversation we overheard at a bait camp between an old retired gentleman and a younger man who sounded like he was visiting from the East Coast. The older of the two was considerably crustier than the Yankee. We were amused that of all the conversation batted around the bait camp, all we heard were emphatic opinions, bottom-line judgments, and unquestionable and irrefutable facts. We also decided that was all right, because that was the stuff that makes bait camps and barber shops unique.

That evening, after way too much of the day's sun, we bemoaned the fact that the world is full of people who would rather grumble and talk than act and do. That was the lesson of the conversation we overheard at the bait camp. Everyone talks about "the Government" and seems to have endless opinions, judgments, and facts to support their position, which is all too often a negative one. We concluded that the talking part is fine, but it's always much better if followed by doing.

This part of Pocket Guide is designed to add more substance to your talk and hopefully motivate you to act on those issues that need your input and support. Government agencies and conservation groups contribute to the preservation of resources we all use. And they do it on a limited budget, usually while under fire from hidden and uninformed groups.

The Texas Parks and Wildlife Department of the State of Texas is a real power in conservation in Texas. In some ways they act like any bureaucracy, subject to the whims of the legislature when it comes to holding the line on wildlife issues important to the state. The commissioners, to whom the members of the Department answer, are appointed by the current Governor. As a commission, they are responsible for making policy decisions and providing guidance to the Department's director.

Parks and Wildlife has an incredible team of professionals, who do a great job for us and the state. As fishermen, we should pay particular attention to the efforts of the people who are responsible for managing the fisheries for the Texas Parks and Wildlife Department. Currently, about 250 technical and administrative professionals operate with an annual budget of more than $10 million. They effectively manage the marine fishery resources of Texas' coastal waters for an estimated 1.6 million fishermen and 10 million consumers, while at the same time preventing depletion and waste. Other accomplishments include an annual census of the finfish, shrimp, crab, and oyster populations, continued updating of scientific resources used to better measure the fish populations, and the preparation of long-range management plans to determine the optimum yield for various species while providing maximum benefits to the fisherman and protection for the fish. They are also heavily involved in restocking all parts of the Texas coast and enhancing the marine habitats by revitalizing existing reefs. The list goes on and on.

As we reviewed all of the programs that are a part of this branch of TP&W, it became quite clear that in spite of the tarnished press, the continuing political battles, and the propensity for all of us to look at them as "government," they do a great job. The best examples of this are our game wardens. These people are saddled with the responsibility of enforcing all the game laws. This enforcement effort guarantees us resources in the future. We should be forever grateful that someone is doing a job that few of us would undertake. The bottom line is, the people at TP&W are our qualified experts. Next time you have a question about why something is the way it is on the Texas coast, ask your expert. We are sure they will bend over backwards to help explain what they are doing to protect the resources of the State of Texas.

The second conservation-oriented group you should be aware of is the Gulf Coast Conservation Association. GCCA is a national organization of outdoor sportsmen and conservationists, most of whom are

volunteers. After more than a decade of involvement in Texas' coasta
waters, they are now recognized for significant contributions in th
areas of education, legislation, and replenishment. As an organization
they have become a model used by other states in developing simila
programs, most of which fall under the CCA umbrella. CCA is a
organization of strong state chapters.

In Texas, GCCA's efforts in education have done more to inform th
public than ever before. One result of this has been an increased leve
of public support for Parks and Wildlife Department proposals to th
legislature. There is nothing like a groundswell of public support t
add credibility to projects requiring legislative funding. Other pro
grams have developed as a result of sportsmen along the coast becomin
more aware of specific problems. For example, Operation Game Thie
rewards citizens who report lawbreakers, and The Coast Watche
program provides training to GCCA members (by Parks and Wildlif
personnel) so that they can observe and report violations on coasta
waters to local state law-enforcement personnel. The Coast Watche
program can have a tremendous effect on how far our game law-en
forcement dollars go because we have a limited number of pai
enforcement officers. In the area of replenishment programs, th
money from GCCA fundraisers, corporate patrons, and institution;
gifts has contributed to making several restocking programs much mo
successful. Thanks to GCCA, Texas Parks and Wildlife, and Centr;
Power and Light, the $6 million GCCA/CPL Marine Developmer
Center in Corpus Christi is now capable of producing up to 20 millio
game-fish fingerlings annually for stocking in Texas waters.

These accomplishments alone put GCCA in a category by itself i
terms of making a difference. We, however, think they should k
recognized for something more important. As an organization, the
have brought pressure to bear in several quarters where historicall
pressure was not the prime motivator. Their method has been
provide a vehicle for dialogue between those groups who share
common interest in the natural resources of Texas. Their involveme
has helped accomplish major goals of those charged with protectir
our resources.

We are the benefactors of their work. Give them your support. F
further information call GCCA: (713) 626-4222.

Another group that may be of interest to you is the Saltwater Anglers League of Texas. S.A.L.T. is a family organization that promotes saltwater fishing, is a source of information for its members, and has even sponsored charity events.

We would like to mention another group, but not because they are well-known conservationists or have contributed in any enormous way to the coastal resources of our state. We mention them because they are good citizens in the field and set a good example for others. As individuals, some of them are involved in GCCA and support various issues affecting our Gulf Coast. As a group, however, they promote the things we think are important: catch and release, respect for the environment, respect for the property of others and, most important, putting something back for future generations. This group does not have a name, but you know who you are. And by the way, keep up the good work!

CHAPTER 6

POTENTIAL PROBLEMS

Hamilton is a friend of ours who used to play professional football. Having fun was never a problem for him because fishing was his true love. Being careful, however, was something he had paid all-too-little attention to, given his reckless life in the NFL. He, and everyone who knew him, considered him to be one of those bullet-proof, invincible types that trouble seemed to avoid.

One day, while fishing a well-known pass, Ham found himself helplessly being drawn under the water by a strong undercurrent. Despite his attempts to regain his footing, he continued to tumble along the bottom until his last breath was no longer enough to sustain the effort to survive.

A week later, the pale-yellow reflected light of a hospital ceiling began to come into focus and Ham realized that he had been spared the cost of a stupid mistake.

Every year, sportsmen along the Gulf Coast either hear about or experience firsthand the effects of an assortment of hazards that can ruin your day on the water, or worst yet, the family you leave behind.

It is our intent to make you aware of several of these hazards and their effects. This list is by no means complete as it only covers a few of the things that can hurt you. Our hope is that you will become much more alert when on the water, and realize how important it is to respect those things that threaten your safety.

Mother Nature

Sun: Even on an overcast day, the sun can sneak up on you and cause enormous belated regret, like when you are on your way home and decide to swing into a convenience store for a cool drink, but first must peel the back of your legs off the vinyl seats in your car. This, of course, is the result of something that gradually happened during the course of the day. Most people only think about the sun and the damage it does to their skin after they have left some of it on the car seat or, even worse, years later when we are forced to pay for our past sins by a bout with skin cancer.

The recommended solutions are in order as follows:

- A good sun-block lotion. We recommend Berkley's Blockaid because it stays on better when you sweat and get wet, and it is formulated for fishermen. For a better sun-blocking effect, we recommend Aloe Gator, which is rated at SPF 40.
- A good hat, which provides shade for your neck and face, and helps regulate body temperature.
- A long-sleeved cotton work shirt. The Sears work shirt is our choice because it is durable, comfortable, and inexpensive.

Weather: The force with which Mother Nature can get our attention is like no other. Whether it's wind, rain, lightning, or any combination of these, when she decides to inflict her fury, we can be made painfully aware that something is about to happen. In spite of her warnings, it seems incredible to us so many people go about their business with total disregard for their own safety. If you were in Kansas or Oklahoma and heard rumor of or actually saw a tornado, you would undoubtedly take shelter. When a water spout is sighted on the coastal areas you fish, you should treat it just as seriously. Water spouts do contain mostly water; unfortunately they also contain an occasional boat, related equipment found on boats, various bait fish (sometimes surrounded by various bait stands), and all kinds of debris picked up as it passed over a peninsula or two, all moving at an incredibly high speed. That's right, high speed. Somehow the U.S. Weather Service measured the wind velocity in one of our local water spouts, and they reported wind velocities up to 130 mph.

If you should see a water spout, please only consider one option: Go in, and consider yourself very lucky to have observed its passing.

Wind also can have unexpected accompanying results. The problem is, wind has an opportunity to increase in velocity as it crosses an expanse of water. The first indication you might notice is a violent gust or two. These are not to be taken lightly because wind gusts have been known to overturn sizable bay boats after their passengers were warned only by an ominous sky.

Lightning: One of the good things about lightning is that it is accompanied by thunder. The purpose of thunder is to make you turn your head away from that bobbing cork and look in the direction of whatever it was that made the noise. Thunder is the result of the almost instantaneous movement of air at supersonic speeds away from a shaft of space that has been created by a tremendous discharge of electrons as they complete a circuit between their source and some point on or connected to the ground. If, by chance, the point on or connected to the ground happens to be a graphite rod, then the holder of said rod dies. We know an ex-fisherman who was hit by lightning. He says, "It really wasn't that bad, at least after my nervous system stopped trying to exit my body through my pores." Why even chance it? *Get out of the water until the thunderstorm moves out of the area.* Here on the coast, most of the summer thunderstorms are of the passing variety anyway and we always say, "Better them than us!"

The following list of things to keep in mind are accurate statements of fact with which no knowledgeable fisherman will argue:

1. A graphite rod is the equivalent of a lightning rod.
2. The boat motor that can power a capsized boat back to the dock has not yet been invented.
3. If you tie in a race with a water spout, you lose.
4. One thing you will never find on the bottom of a pass is a life vest.

Life is too short to take chances with Mother Nature—you may only get to lose once.

Critters (or, the things war stories are made of)

Jellyfish: We have no idea how many kinds of jellyfish there are in the world. What we do know is there are two on the Gulf Coast that we think can cause you problems. One is the cabbage head jellyfish. Because of the reputation shared by all critters that have the capacity to hurt you, the cabbage head is perceived to be more of a threat than it really is. Most people hurt themselves trying to get out of its way. If you happen to touch the trailing end of a cabbage head, you will experience some stinging, but certainly not unmanageable pain.

The other variety, the Portuguese man-of-war, is another story. We think of this one as the jalapeño of saltwater, except that you never get used to its sting. They are generally observed on top of the water and look like inflated blueish-lavender balloons with trailing thread-like appendages. These appendages extend several feet behind the Portuguese man-of-war, and are used to sting or otherwise render its prey helpless. Any contact made between this jellyfish and a fisherman's skin will result in extraordinary pain. Therefore, dealing with these critters is simple. Avoid contact with them by wearing clothing that covers your skin. If you are stung by a jellyfish, there are readily available medications your doctor can give you for just such situations.

Hardhead Catfish: The hardhead catfish is armed with several protruding spines that can cause a serious puncture wound. As is the case with many saltwater species, this fish offers a bonus in the form of a toxic substance accompanying the puncture wound, virtually guaranteeing additional pain and oftentimes an infection. We recommend seeing a doctor as soon as possible after an encounter with a hardhead, and know of no one who has experienced this pain who would disagree with us.

The best protection against hardheads is a healthy respect and a large pair of needle-nose pliers. If you catch a hardhead, hold the curved part of the hook with the pliers and flip the fish back off of the barb. Since this is sometimes no easy task, it's a good idea to perform this operation at arm's length, as a dropped hardhead can cause additional problems with ill-positioned feet.

Sharks: To most fishermen, the order of fish on a stringer goes something like this: speckled trout, speckled trout, flounder, speckled trout, redfish, redfish, speckled trout. To a shark, however, it's more like: speckled trout, speckled trout, ankle, redfish, speckled kneebone, flounder, thigh. It seems the poor critters get confused in and among all that meat, and that is usually when the problems occur. Sharks (and other fish as well) are attracted to sounds and vibrations in the water. We have observed that one of the most effective sound and vibration generators known to man is a fisherman who has just experienced a shark swimming between his legs in 4 feet of water. All too often a fisherman cannot successfully attain the required airspeed to lift himself out of the water by simply flailing his arms at humming-bird speed, and so resorts to the old Mississippi-paddle-boat method.

There is, of course, another approach. When confronted by a situation involving sharks, remember you are in his domain. He has the advantage of speed and cover. All he is doing is looking for food. If you have already cornered a meal for him, he will most certainly show his appreciation by beheading your catch (and leaving them for you). That 15-foot stringer we recommend should allow you to observe the entire act at a safe distance. As you are untying it, remember the stringer is so easy and inexpensive to replace and rarely requires recovery time in the hospital.

Boating Safety

1. Motorless craft have the right-of-way in almost all cases. Sailing vessels and motorboats less than 65 feet long shall not hamper, in a narrow channel, the safe passage of a vessel which can navigate only inside that channel.

2. A motorboat being overtaken has the right-of-way.

3. Motorboats approaching head to head (or nearly so) should pass port to port.

4. When motorboats approach each other at right angles or obliquely, the boat on the right has the right-of-way in most cases.

5. Motorboats must keep to the right in narrow channels, when safe and practicable.

Mariners are urged to become familiar with the complete text of the *Rules of the Road* in the U.S. Coast Guard publication "Navigation Rules."

We have always considered the most important piece of equipment on a boat to be the operator. Use your head and let common sense prevail. Remember, you are driving the equivalent of a full-size car with no brakes. So, allow yourself plenty of time to deal with any situation.

CHAPTER 7

SPECIAL APPLICATIONS

COLD WEATHER FISHING

Cold weather fishing falls into two basic types. The first is fishing from a boat over a deep hole where the fish were driven by the low tides and cold water temperatures associated with Texas' blue northers. The second is wading the flats in search of monster speckled trout. This technique is used after the front has blown itself out, and the clear skies and bright sun associated with the high pressure behind the storm have had 3 or 4 days to warm the flats. This waiting period is also necessary to allow the tide levels to return to normal to bring a sufficient stand of water back to the flats. We will discuss each of these in detail.

Hole fishing is best as soon as possible after the blow or when the area offers sufficient protection to allow you to get there. The water temperature will be in the high 40s to 50s. Fish are cold-blooded, meaning their body temperature approximates that of their environment. This brutal cold slows the metabolism of the fish and they become lethargic. They move slowly and conserve their energy. The fish are extremely different in their feeding habits from the speckled trout that viciously slam your offering in the spring and summer. They will remain motionless, out of any current, and wait for their next meal to present itself. When they take a bait drifting by it will be only a slight tap or dead weight, like hitting a snag. A graphite rod and sharp hooks are necessary to feel the hit and set the hook. Most of these fish

104

will be lip-hooked, requiring a taut-line retrieve and a light hook set. A landing net is a necessity to avoid loosing the fish at boatside.

Presentation of the bait is the key. It must be worked very, very slowly and with the current, if any. Reducing your mechanical advantage by using a reel with a lower gear ratio will assist you in maintaining this slow retrieve. That old reel may be just the ticket in this situation. The fish will not move far to take your bait. They will go with the current to get the bait, but never against. The fish will use bottom structure to block the current while they wait, facing into the current. Deep-running hard plastic baits are used, but we prefer to use soft plastic baits. Two reasons for this are, first, the fish will hold onto a soft bait longer before rejecting it because it feels right and, second, a single hook is less likely to end up on the junk littering the bottom than are the two or three treble hooks of hard baits.

Deep-water havens for cold weather fishing include the Galveston Ship Channel between Pelican Island and Lower Galveston Bay; the deep hole between Smith Point and Eagle Point; the two holes on the north side of Moses Lake; Conn Brown Harbor at Port Aransas; the Army Hole at Port O'Connor; the Intracoastal Canal; the Jetties at Sabine Pass, Galveston, and Port O'Connor; Chocolate Bayou; the Texas City Turning Basin; Offatts Bayou; the hole off the HL&P's Bacliff warm-water discharge canal; and the Colorado River. These last three deserve special attention.

Offatts Bayou

Offatts Bayou was once a shallow, meandering bayou in the heart of Galveston. The fill necessary for the grade-raising of the city of Galveston and construction of the seawall transformed the Bayou into a deep-water shelter for fish, averaging 18- to 20-feet deep with holes up to 40 feet. During severe winters, it offers easy limits to the properly-clothed fisherman. Mild winters will not cause the water to cool sufficiently, nor the requisite drop in water level in West Bay to drive the fish into the Bayou. A water temperature in the high 40s is required to concentrate the fish there. Timing is also important. Offatts is well protected, and can (and should) be fished immediately after the height of the norther has blown through. The first day after a norther with bright sun is the time to hit it. December and January are the big trout months. A boat with an electronic depth finder is the way to find the deep holes, and that is where the fish will be.

Some of the areas to hit at Offatts are as follows: The Blue Hole off the east shoreline of the Airport at 20 to 24 feet; both sides of Long Reef, which runs down the middle of the Bayou north of the Airport; the drop-off at High Grade Hole on the northeast shoreline at 20 feet; and the hole off Race Track Point on the northeast corner at 25 feet. Remember, patience! Let the lure sink to the bottom and work it slowly. If the fish are suspended, use the countdown method to try different depths until the right one is found. White is a popular lure color; the 51 MirrOlure or white and pearl-firetail KelleyWigglers are good.

Bacliff Spillway Discharge Canal

The Houston Lighting and Power Company's Robinson Station discharges water used to cool its generators through this canal into upper Galveston Bay. This 80° water flowing into the cold waters of the Bay attracts schools of speckled trout and redfish. The canal discharge area can be fished from both banks, from a lighted pier adjacent to the canal, or the adjoining shorelines can be waded. Bank fishermen cast into the current and drift their bait with the flow to the waiting game fish. The added warmth of the discharge rejuvenates the fish and provides hot action in the coldest months. Because of the rocks and miscellaneous junk on the bottom, use single hook baits and be prepared to loose some equipment. In calm weather small boats can also fish the discharge canal, with a launching ramp located at the mouth of the canal. More on the Spillway Fishing Pier is included later in this chapter.

Colorado River

Cold weather moves the fish from West Matagorda, and particularly the shallower East Matagorda, into the deeper water of the Colorado River. Fish can be found from the mouth of the river up to 15 miles upstream depending upon the volume of fresh water coming down the river. Because this is river fishing, the current plays a major role in finding the fish. The fish will be in the holes where the humps, ridges, and debris afford them shelter from the current. The trick is to find these holes, some of which are 20-feet deep or more, and then position the boat so that you can cast upstream and let the current wash your offering into the hole (or at least by the hole). The fish will swim with the current to catch the bait and run back to the hole out of the current. The holes may actually be valleys between ridges on the bottom—anything to block the current. Your boat's electronic depth finder is the key to finding the area. Drift it and see if you pick up anything. Let your bait drift with the current. If you connect, come back through and anchor to continue working the area.

Shad-type soft plastic baits are excellent in the Colorado. Use 3/8 - or possibly 1/2 -oz jig heads to get the lure to the bottom. Hogie Swimming Jacks in red/pink tail, black/white tail, and night glow are good colors. Red works best in clear water with the darker colors working best in off-color water. Locate the structure, get the bait to the bottom, and fish with the current, and the Colorado River can mean hot fishing in the cold weather.

The other cold weather fishing is for big speckled trout on the flats. For the flats to be productive, a number of factors have to be in your favor. It is these factors which bring the fish onto the flats. Timing is critical. As always, you have to be there when the fish are, and in the winter they may be there one day and gone the next. The speckled trout prefer a water temperature above 55° to get out onto the flats. The range of 55° to 68° is prime. You also need to be on a shoreline protected from the wind, have an incoming tide (the bigger the better) or an outgoing tide after a big high tide, and, the ever-present qualifier, bait in the water.

These fish are not the same ones that you had to hit in the nose with your lure to catch in the deep holes. These fish are on the flats eating mullet, and, as such, will be looking for a fast-moving prey. No more slow retrieve. Fast retrieves and frequent jerks from the rod tip are the way to go here. These fish will probably not be schooled. The tactic is to fan out, make long casts, and cover a lot of ground to find the fish. Key in on the mullet. Work guts, canals, and open flats to find the fish. Proximity to channels or other deep water is another key to selecting which flats to work. Between northers, after several days of sunshine to warm the flats, is when to go. If you are looking for that wall hanger, you have to be prepared to do a lot of walking and a lot of casting, with maybe only one or two strikes a day. This is not fast action, but you are also not after a 14-inch fish. Trophy fish come to the wader who pays his dues by being there and working for it.

Productive shorelines include Dollar Flats south to the Texas City Dike; Kemah shoreline to Eagle Point; Seabrook Flats; McCullom Park to the HL&P Spillway Channel in Trinity Bay; Vingt-Et-Un Island to the Anahuac Channel in Trinity Bay; Eagle Point to April Fool Point; Rooster Collins Flats in West Bay to Bay Harbor; Sea Isle to Anderson Ways in West Bay; Baffle Point to Sievers Cut in East Bay; Sievers Cut to Fat Rat Pass; Frozen Point in East Bay; North Flats in Trinity Bay; and Umbrella Point to Cedar Point in Trinity Bay. The most effective MirrOlure colors include 801, 11, CF, SHP, 51, 704, 752, and 24. Winter wading for a trophy is hard work, but reliving the tale to your friends in front of the mount will definitely dull the pain and agony.

NIGHT WADEFISHING

The primary differences between wadefishing at night and during the day are two. First, it is dark—very dark. Second, different lures are used. The first of these is significant in a number of ways. Night wading is the means to take advantage of prime fishing times usually missed, and yes, speckled trout are caught at night without fish-attracting lights. It can, however, be dangerous. It is for the expert wader who has an expert-wader friend. *Do not wade at night alone.* If you get in trouble, no help will be available. Only wade at night in areas with which you are thoroughly familiar from day fishing. Even at this, it will be different at night. The Seabrook and Kemah Flats are good choices, as are the Dollar Flats. As you can tell from these locations, do not wade at night around passes or areas with strong currents. If you travel by boat to your wade location, exercise extreme caution and do so slowly. Crab pots and pilings are much easier to locate in the light. (We truly believe that someone moves these at night, anyway. They are never where they are supposed to be.) Warm clothing and a parka or wind breaker are required well into the summer. Extra clothes should be available when wearing waders. Reflective tape should be worn on your outer clothing to ensure that you are seen by boaters using spot lights. Advise someone of where you are going to wade and when you intend to be back, and stick to the plan.

At night you plan your trip based upon the same variables that you use during the day. To these add the moon phases. Obviously, a full moon will light up the area under clear skies and provide good tides. A new moon will provide these same tides. Three days on either side of both are prime fishing periods for big fish. Night wading can be done with live bait under a popping cork or on the bottom. Live bait does, however, limit your mobility and, as such, we prefer to wade with lures. The belly boaters have also scored in the dark, and probably work well with live bait. Night lures are usually black because they silhouette best against the sky, making them more visible. We also use lures that rattle. We use the following: MirrOlures in 52MR54, 52MR807, 52MRNS, and 97MRNS, Cotton Cordell broken-back Redfins in silver/black back, and the Zara Spook in black.

The last and final piece of equipment should go without saying: a flashlight. We carry a regular-sized flashlight and wear a small light on our hats. This allows us to tie knots, untangle lines, clean debris from our lures, stringer fish, and try to find what just brushed against our legs while leaving our hands free to fish or perform the required task. Play it safe, and night wading can turn into quite an experience. You can even catch fish doing it!

SURF FISHING

Surf fishing is unique more from what happens to the fisherman than what the fisherman can catch. The surf is in no way similar to the calm wading of a bay's protected shoreline, except on the two days when the wind is not blowing. All the rest of the time, the waves can be very punishing and dangerous. Surf wading near a major pass can be absolutely death-defying and should be attempted only by expert swimmers. The third bar, or more exactly the deep water on the other side of the third bar, is where it is widely believed the fish usually are. It takes supreme willpower to stay safely on the second bar and catch a few fish while watching the daredevils catch a bunch of fish from the third bar. But, that is exactly what most of us should do. The average fisherman should not be on the third bar except in the calmest of conditions. On high tides, the second gut frequently has the fish. At first light on an incoming tide, the fish may be in the first gut. Only on outgoing or minimal incoming tides is it the third bar where we consistently find the action.

Our rigs were designed to withstand the abuse of the surf and are overequipped for the bays. We use ski rope with heavy-duty snaps, heavy-duty split rings, and leather or synthetic sheaths for our tools, with lines attached to the tools themselves to ensure retrieval if and when they are dropped. Our wading belts have evolved from years of abuse (and from having at one time or another lost almost everything carried on them) into a system that stays together and provides the equipment needed when we wade. In the surf the rule is that you will loose everything that is not tied down, and half the stuff that is.

The Galveston Island shoreline from the South Jetty to San Luis Pass, the Bolivar Peninsula surf from above High Island to the North Jetty, and the Folletts Island surf from San Luis Pass to the Freeport Jetties all have the potential to provide excellent surf fishing. The wind is the key. Southeast winds at 10 knots or less gives the surf wader the "trout green" water he needs. Find green water with bait on an incoming tide and get after it. The MirrOlure 52MR28 is a killer in the surf. We also like the 1¼-oz Tony Accetta spoon in gold and silver. The extra weight make these spoons cast like a bullet. We use bucktails in these occasionally, white/silver and red/gold. Spanish Mackerel love these spoons with white bucktails. If they are present, a 6-in. steel leader will be required to protect your hardware.

PIER FISHING

Pier fishing is a broad topic since almost every type of fish found in the Gulf of Mexico has, at one time or another, been caught from a pier in Texas. This usually happens off one of the large commercial piers that jut out into the Gulf 1,000 yards or more. We, however, will discuss the techniques involved in catching speckled trout from a pier, and not just a 1,000-foot monster. The pier behind your beach house, or that of your friend (it is always advisable that this person *know* he is your friend), can also be productive if it is in proximity to either the bays or the Gulf.

Most speckled trout are caught off piers in the summer at night using high-powered floodlights aimed at the water. The lights shining into the water attract flying bugs and small marine organisms, which are the bottom of the food chain. These attract the smaller fish and so on and so forth. The best conditions are clear water and an incoming tide. Schools of speckled trout cruising the area will move in and out of the lights to feed.

Pay attention to what you see in the lights as this will dictate the bait to use. Most popular is live shrimp; however, if the trout are scooping bugs off the surface, a tiny beetle in clear glitter is a killer. We use KelleyWigglers in white, pearl, and clear glitter, and small shad-type plastics, again in clear glitter. The 52MR11 MirrOlure also works as does the 52MRS and 52MR51. The speckled trout will be in shallow water. On the big piers, check out the lights in 4 to 6 feet of water, not out on the T-head. Watch the wave action and find the second or third bar—the corresponding guts will be where the fish are. What the fish are chasing and where will determine the proper bait and depth at which to fish.

A fish-finder rig is best for bottom-feeding fish, a cork or Mansfield Mauler for suspended fish, and free shrimp or a weightless hook on the top for surface feeders. The Mansfield Mauler also works on surface-feeding speckled trout. Keep your bait moving to cover the area and make it more visible to the fish. Cast into the darkness and bring your bait back into the light. Speckled trout will be visible darting in the bright light, but we get more strikes out near the edge of the light. Piers can present a problem in landing a fish. Small trout, particularly when using live bait, can be hoisted up over the rail most of the time. The proper technique is to lower your rod, reeling in sufficient line. Then, in a single smooth motion, hoist the fish over the rail. This will not work with a larger fish. Artificials usually result in a lip hook which will tear out more times than not. Any speckled trout that you really want should be netted. A long handled net should be part of your equipment. On the larger commercial piers, long-handled nets are sometimes available. Some people use what we call a "basket net" that is lowered over the railing on a cord. It has a framework that keeps it open. It is lowered below the surface and the fish is drawn onto the net. It is then raised up, catching the fish, and brought back up over the rail.

Following is a list of the piers available on the Texas Coast. Call them to check on availability of live bait, nets, etc.

TEXAS FISHING PIERS

Meacom's Pier: Bolivar Peninsula, on the Gulf, 2 miles from High Island. (409) 266-5675

Dirty Pelican Pier: Bolivar Peninsula, on the Gulf, east of Gilchrist. (409) 286-5854

Seawolf Park Pier: Pelican Island across the Galveston Ship Channel from Galveston Island, on Lower Galveston Bay. (409) 744-5738

Texas City Lighted Pier: At the end of the Texas City Dike, on Lower Galveston Bay. (409) 948-8171

18th Street Fishing Pier: San Leon, on Upper Galveston Bay. (713) 339-2600

Spillway Pier: Bacliff, on Upper Galveston Bay at the HL&P discharge canal. (713) 599-2403

Flagship Hotel Pier: Galveston Island, on the Gulf. (409) 762-9000

61st Street Pier: Galveston Island, on the Gulf. (409) 744-8365

Gulf Coast Pier: Galveston Island, on the Gulf. (409) 744-2273

San Luis Pass Fishing Pier: Follets Island at San Luis Pass, on the Gulf. (409) 233-6902

Lavaca State Fishing Pier: Port Lavaca, on Lavaca Bay. (512) 522-4402

Copano Pass Fishing Pier: East of Rockport/Fulton, on Copano Bay. (512) 729-8566

Bob Hall Pier: North end of Padre Island, on the Gulf. (512) 949-8425

Horace Coldwell Pier: Padre Island at Port Isabel, on the Laguna Madre. (512) 561-9807

Each of these piers has its own personality. Call ahead to determine what they are catching and their rules regarding amount of tackle per person. Also, ask them how high above the water the pier sits. This information will help you plan how to land the big one.

APPENDIX

RECOMMENDED GUIDES

Sabine Lake and vicinity—
Jerry Norris	(409) 736-3023
Ernie Eickenhorst	(409) 722-1592

Galveston Bay and vicinity—
Bolivar Guide Service	(409) 684-7162
Jim West	
Tarpon Express Guide Service	(713) 723-1911
Mike Williams	
Mickey Eastman Guide Service	(713) 383-2737
Mickey Eastman	
Campbell Guide Service	(713) 421-4560
Bob Campbell	
Mrs. L.U. "Cookie" Pepper Guide Service	(409) 737-1136
"Cookie" Pepper	
Darrell Skillern Guide Service	(713) 426-6449
Darrell Skillern	
Friermood's Guide Service	(713) 427-7923
Blaien Friermood	or (713) 422-9655
James Plaag Guide Service	(713) 446-3918
James Plaag	

Gulf Coast Guide Service	(713) 487-1369
Windy Marshall	
Charlie Paradoski Guide Service	(713) 495-9084
Charlie Paradoski	
Chris Phillips Guide Service	(713) 370-6842
Chris Phillips	
Frazier's Guide Service	(713) 339-1685
Ralph Frazier	
We're Gone Fishing Guide Service	(409) 945-0672
David Wright	
Harry Landers Guide Service	(409) 737-1037
Harry Landers	
Dave's Guide Service	(409) 233-7226
Dave Kreton	or (409) 684-3071

Matagorda Bays and vicinity—

Bob Gardner Guide Service	(409) 863-2149
Bob Gardner	or (713) 772-4502
Charles Shafer Guide Service	(409) 245-5017
Charles Shafer	
Tarpon Express Guide Service	(713) 723-1911
Mike Williams	
Matagorda Charterboats	(409) 863-7434
Raymond Cox	

Port O'Connor and vicinity—

Red Childers Guide Service	(512) 983-2937
Red Childers	
Robbie Gregory Guide Service	(512) 983-2862
Robbie Gregory	
Steve Pfuntner Guide Service	(512) 983-4447
Steve Pfuntner	

FISHING CHECK LIST

Fishing license with Saltwater Stamp and other identification
    (drivers license)
Rods (with tips)
Reels
Wading Belt with Attachments
Life Vest
Net(s)
Waders or Wading Shoes
Fanny Pack
Tackle Box(es)
Cooler(s)
Extra Lures
Insect Spray
Sun Block
Polarized Sunglasses
Hat
Weather Radio
Extra Clothes
Rain Gear
Bucket(s)
Cast Net
Aerator
Battery
Bait
Bait Bucket(s)
Chair(s)
Camera with Film
Other Stuff Not Previously Itemized (like a garbage sack for wet
    clothes)
A Fishing Buddy; preferably a young fishing buddy (if you don't
    have one, borrow one!)

EMERGENCY NUMBERS

PORT ARTHUR

U.S. Coast Guard (Sabine Pass)	(409) 766-5620
Jefferson County Sheriff	(409) 835-8411
Port Arthur Police	(409) 983-8600
Texas Parks & Wildlife (Beaumont)	(409) 892-8666

GALVESTON

U.S. Coast Guard (Galveston)	(409) 766-5620
U.S. Coast Guard Air Station (Ellington)	(713) 481-0025
Galveston County Sheriff (Galveston)	(409) 766-2222
(Marine Division)	(409) 766-2222
(Dickinson Area)	(713) 534-3516
Galveston Police	(409) 766-2100
Texas Parks & Wildlife (Galveston)	(409) 762-0732
(LaPorte)	(409) 471-3202
Texas City Police	(409) 948-2525
Harris County Sheriff	(713) 221-6000

MATAGORDA

Matagorda County Sheriff	(409) 245-5526

PORT O'CONNOR

U.S. Coast Guard (Port O'Connor)	(512) 983-2616
Calhoun County Sheriff	(512) 553-4646
Port O'Connor Police	(512) 553-4646
Texas Parks & Wildlife (Matagorda Island)	(512) 552-5688

ALL AREAS

AAA Emergency Number (in Texas)	(800) 392-4353

TIDAL DIFFERENCES CHART

The National Oceanic and Atmospheric Administration has produced a chart that accurately predicts high- and low-tide information. On the Texas coast, a tide measurement at the Galveston jetties, where the tides are measured, may not coincide with tidal movement of water several miles away (where you happen to be fishing). The Tidal Differences Chart shows you in hours and minutes just how much you must adjust the time shown for a high or low tide.

PLACE	HIGH	LOW
Sabine Bank Lighthouse	– 1:46	– 1:31
Sabine Pass (Jetty)	– 1:26	– 1:31
Sabine Pass	– 1:00	– 1:15
Mesquite Point, Sabine Pass	– 0:04	– 0:25
Galveston Bay entrance, S. Jetty	– 0:39	– 1:05
Port Bolivar	+ 0:14	– 0:06
GALVESTON CHANNEL	` AS SHOWN	
Galveston Bay		
Texas City, Turning Basin	+ 0:33	+ 0:41
Eagle Point	+ 3:54	+ 4:15
Morgans Point	+ 10:21	+ 5:19
Point Barrow, Trinity Bay	+ 5:48	+ 4:43
Gilchrist, East Bay	+ 3:16	+ 4:18
Jamaica Beach, West Bay	+ 2:38	+ 3:31
Alligator Point, West Bay	+ 2:39	+ 2:33
Christmas Point, Christmas Bay	+ 2:32	+ 2:31
San Luis Pass	– 0:09	– 0:09
Freeport Harbor	– 0:44	– 1:02
Pass Cavallo	0:00	– 1:20
Port O'Connor, Matagorda Bay	+ 0:34	– 0:46

INDEX

118

Other titles you'll enjoy from Lone Star Books/Gulf Publishing Company:

- Pocket Guide to Speckled Trout and Redfish: South Texas Coast Edition
- Mariner's Atlas: Texas Gulf Coast
- A Beachcomber's Guide to Gulf Coast Marine Life
- The Book of Marine Fishes
- A Guide to Texas Rivers and Streams
- Camper's Guide to Texas Parks, Lakes, and Forests
- Eyes of Texas: Houston/Gulf Coast
- Hiking and Backpacking Trails of Texas